Joseph Harris

Gardening for Young and Old

The cultivation of garden vegetables in the farm garden

Joseph Harris

Gardening for Young and Old
The cultivation of garden vegetables in the farm garden

ISBN/EAN: 9783337068943

Printed in Europe, USA, Canada, Australia, Japan

Cover: Foto ©Lupo / pixelio.de

More available books at **www.hansebooks.com**

GARDENING
FOR
YOUNG AND OLD.

THE
CULTIVATION OF GARDEN VEGETABLES
IN THE FARM GARDEN.

BY

JOSEPH HARRIS, M.S.,

AUTHOR OF "WALKS AND TALKS ON THE FARM," "HARRIS ON THE PIG,"
"TALKS ON MANURES," ETC.

ILLUSTRATED.

NEW YORK:
ORANGE JUDD COMPANY,
751 BROADWAY.
1883.

CONTENTS.

	PAGE
Introduction	7
An Old and a New Garden	8
Gardening for Boys	9
How to Begin	10
Preparing the Soil	12
Killing the Weeds	13
About High Farming	15
Competition in Crops	17
The Manure Question	19
The Implements Needed	21
Starting Plants in the House, or in the Hot-bed	22
Making the Hot-bed	25
Cold Frames	26
Insects	26
The Use of Poisons	27
The Care of Poisons	30
The Cultivation of Vegetables in the Farm-garden	31
The Cultivation of Flowers	150

PREFACE.

I should like to see more seed-growers in the United States, and I hope some of my young friends will devote themselves to this industry. There are more seeds sown in America, in proportion to population, than in any other country. European seedsmen, notwithstanding a duty of twenty per cent., find the United States one of the best markets in the world.

It seems to be a fact, that many seeds, when grown here, produce much better crops than when grown in Europe. Market gardeners give a decided preference to American-grown seeds. American-grown cabbage seeds, for instance, find a ready sale at double the price of imported seed.

Cauliflower seed has hitherto rarely been grown in this country successfully, but I understand that California is now growing it of excellent quality. Dakota is growing cabbage seed, and I feel confident that somewhere on this broad Continent, with its great diversity of soil and climate, there is not a seed which the American gardener wants, that will not be grown to perfection. The great point is to get what seed-growers call "stock seed," to start with. As a rule, you can not buy it. You must grow it yourself. Take Cucumber seed, for example. Enormous quantities of Cucumber seed are grown and sold in America, and yet it is exceedingly difficult to get good seed, pure, and true to name. And so of Watermelon seed. A gentleman in Barnwell, S. C., wrote me a few days ago for Watermelon seed, for his own use, sufficient to plant one hundred and fifty acres. Such a man could afford to pay a high price for seed, that was known to be good, rather than to accept common seed as a gift. Seedsmen, as a rule, are honorable men, and would cheerfully pay good prices to a careful seed-grower, whose seeds always proved to be as represented.

I would particularly urge some of my young friends to turn their attention to seed-growing. They should make it the business of their lives, and the earlier they commence, the better. They need the best of education, the highest moral character, a good stock of patience and common sense, the best of land, and above all, a hopeful disposition, that will enable them to persevere amid manifold discouragements. I know of no industry which promises greater success. None of us, however, wish to see American Horticulture degenerate into a money-making business. It is preëminently worthy of attention for its refining and ennobling influence. I have often thought of the words of Hooker, written more than three hundred years ago: "The beauty of trees when we behold them, delighteth the eye." The beauty of flowers elevates the taste, and their cultivation gives health and pleasure. J. H.

GARDENING FOR YOUNG AND OLD.

INTRODUCTION.

I first thought of calling this book "Gardening for Young Folks," but I found that the young folks of my intimate acquaintance, and who are as much interested in the book as any one else is likely to be, very decidedly objected to the title. And it was at their suggestion that I decided to call it "Gardening for Young and Old"—with a mental reservation that it should be principally for the Young Folks.

The fact is, the children are right. It is not "Gardening for Young Folks" alone that is required. The young would do little without the advice and sympathy and encouragement of their fathers and mothers, or older friends. And some old folks I know are almost as bad, or worse. They can do little or nothing in the garden unless they have the young people to help them. The fact is, the Old were made for the Young, and the Young were made for the Old.

I know an old farmer who has given up the active management of his farm, and who devotes his whole time to the garden. It is a small garden, but it is a model of neatness and thorough cultivation. Not a weed, or a stone, or a stick, is to be found in it; he has the earliest of vegetables and the sweetest of flowers. But there is not enough to it, his garden is simply a plaything, but it has done one good thing. One of his grandchildren, a bright active boy, has a decided taste for gardening.

He sometimes visits me and takes a deep interest in all that is going on. He is willing to learn, is not afraid of work, and he is ready to adopt a new plan. If his father would give him the chance, and the grandfather aid him with his experience (as he will), this young man will soon have a garden that is a garden; in fact, he has already commenced. He has enclosed about an acre of land near the barn-yard, and adjoining the old garden. It may not be big enough, but it will do to commence with. This young man has been frequently in my mind while writing this book.

AN OLD AND A NEW GARDEN.

I want to introduce a new system of gardening. I do not wish to do away with the old gardens, but I would see new ones on every farm. Moreover, I want to see them big enough to admit of the use of the plow, the harrow, the roller, and above all, of the horse-hoe, for cultivating between the rows of growing plants. I have myself just such a garden, and I have also an old-fashioned garden, full of trees, and walks, and bushes, and—weeds. There are two or three beds of asparagus that do not amount to much. In one corner there is a' mass of horse-radish, and along the fence there is a row of currant bushes. There was formerly a score or more of English gooseberries, but the mildew and the Saw-fly have been too much for them. We have grapevines growing vigorously, and here and there a bed of beautiful roses. There are beds of thyme, sage, rosemary, parsley, and rhubarb. The latter produces an abundance of seed, but only a few somewhat stringy stalks. This bed of rhubarb stands right across a strip of land where, but for it, I could use a cultivator to great advantage. We have peach trees, cherry trees, pear trees, raspberries, blackberries, and strawberry beds. In short, it is a large, old-fashioned garden. It is no worse than many others, and better than some gardens. Trees that I planted with my own hands are now fifty feet high. Rows of dwarf apple trees, on each side of a twenty-foot walk, in spite of all the pruning we could give them, interlock their branches. I would not destroy the old garden. It has been a source of much pleasure, and it is still not without its attractive features. But there is not a crop in it that does not cost more than it is worth. In spite of all the hoeing we can give it, by the time we are through with the harvest the garden is full of weeds.

I have another garden, several acres in extent, with only a fence between it and the old garden, to which it presents a decided contrast. I will not boast, but I think there are more weeds on a square rod in many parts of the old garden than could be found on a whole acre of the new. This is simply because we have room enough for all the modern tools for preparing the land, drilling in the seed, and cultivating the crops. Wherever the plow and the cultivator can be used, we get good crops, and clean land, and if not, not.

GARDENING FOR BOYS.

I want to interest the boys in gardening. I would like to have them start with new land and new methods. Select the best piece of land you have. I do not care how big it is. Three or four acres is none too much. The amount of work required will depend on the kind of crops to be raised; you can raise an acre of sweet corn, or an acre of early potatoes, or an acre of late cabbages, with half the labor required to raise an acre of onions. Let the garden be big enough, and if you fear you can not command sufficient labor to grow the more expensive crops, then devote the larger portion of the ground to those crops which can be kept clean almost entirely by the use of the cultivator, and aim to have some of the crops come in early, and some to mature late, so that all the work of gathering the crops will not have to be done at one time.

Even if you are sure of the labor, it is a good plan at first to grow crops with which you are most familiar, and which do not require excessively rich land. It takes some years to get land in the very best condition for many of our best garden crops. Even such a common crop as early cabbages will do better on land that has been heavily manured two or three years, and occupied each year with cabbages, than can be grown on new land, no matter how heavily it may be manured. The same is true of onions; old onion land, provided it is well manured every year, is proverbially better for this crop than new land.

I want the boys to engage in gardening, because they are young and can afford to wait, but more especially because they will be more likely to adopt new processes, and will be willing to bestow the necessary care and labor in preparing the land. I can not insist too much on the importance of this matter, not only at first, but in the years to come.

HOW TO BEGIN.

If the land selected for a garden is not naturally well, drained, it must be under-drained. Without this, success is impossible. Fall plowing is of great importance, and I do not mean by this simply turning over the soil with a plow, and letting the furrows lie undisturbed until spring. If it is sod-land, it should be plowed deep and well, as early as possible, and the surface afterwards harrowed and rolled, cultivated and again rolled, and harrowed again, until there are four or five inches of loose mellow soil. If the plowing was done so early that the sod is so rotted that it can be cross-plowed before winter sets in, all the better. It can not be plowed too often in the fall. All stones and rubbish must be removed.

ABOUT MANURES.

The application of manure is no doubt a very important matter, but in many cases a still more important one is, how to get the manure. We never have all we could use to advantage. Unless we buy manure, we must rob some other part of the farm in order to enrich the garden. Most farmers will be startled at this proposition. In many cases, however, it is the true plan. A farmer with a hundred acres of land could use all the manure he makes on a ten-acre field devoted to garden crops. He could use phosphates on the farm, and manure and phosphates in the garden. On the farm he could enrich his land by summer-fallowing and plowing under green crops. The more stock he keeps, and the more grass, corn, oats, peas, mustard, rape, and millet he grows and consumes on the farm, the more manure he will make. In many cases he could with advantage buy food to feed his stock.

My own plan is, to rot the manure by making it into heaps five feet wide and about five feet high, and of any desired length. It is piled in the barn-yard as fast as it is made. In the winter we draw these piles into the field where the manure is to be used, and make it into other piles five feet wide and five feet high, as before, being careful to carry the heaps up straight and square, so that the top shall be as wide as the bottom. If you do not insist on this being done, the teamsters will make the heap like the roof of a house, and before spring the manure will be frozen solid. On the other hand, if the heap is carefully made, the manure will decompose and keep warm, and be in splendid condition for use early in the spring.

PREPARING THE SOIL.

In preparing land for a garden, as before said, we can not plow it too much in the autumn. If the land can not be got into good condition in the fall, it certainly can not be done in the spring. This is true not only of new land, but of old garden land. Said an old gardener and seed-grower to me the other day: "The longer I live, the more am I convinced of the importance of fall plowing. It makes the land cleaner, and you are ready to commence work much earlier in the spring."

I know a farmer who wished to make a large field-garden, who selected a good piece of land, and plowed it up in the spring and sowed it to buckwheat, and when the crop was in flower, he plowed it under and seeded it again to buckwheat. He had an immense crop, but he managed with a good plow and chain to turn it under. He then, in August, or the first of September, sowed the land to rye, and the next spring, about the middle of May, he plowed under the rye. The land was wonderfully mellow and full of vegetable matter, and he had a grand piece of land on which to commence gardening operations. By the aid of a little phosphate it is easy to grow good sweet corn, melons, cucumbers, beets, and late cabbages on such land.

Gardeners who live near a city where land is high, will think they can not afford to let their land lie idle. They will prefer to buy manure rather than plow under green crops. But in the country, where we wish to start a field-garden, and can not buy manure, there can be little doubt but that we can very cheaply enrich the land by plowing under such crops as buckwheat, white mustard, and rye. I do not say that we can make land very rich in this way, but we can fill it full of vegetable mould, and at the same time make the soil clean and mellow. The system of gardening I wish to advocate in the country is based on the idea of having a large garden, only a part of which is necessarily occupied by crops which require a maximum amount of manure. I want the garden so large from the start, that the whole of it may be very thoroughly plowed and subdued and brought into good shape, and be ready at any time to receive such garden crops as we may wish to grow.

It will do a farmer good—it will certainly do his boys good—to have such a piece of land or field, where the very best system of cultivation is adopted. Very few farmers know what really good cultivation means. I am myself a farmer, and the son and grandson and great-grandson of a farmer, and mean no disrespect to farmers when I say that most of us have very little idea of how much land can be improved by thorough cultivation and high manuring.

KILLING THE WEEDS.

The first year I came upon the farm where I now live, there was a field of ten acres of wheat. The field was seeded to clover, but the clover was killed out, and the wheat stubble was one mass of Quack-grass. I had had considerable experience with this under-ground weed, and I was determined to kill it, and I did kill it. The field to-day is occupied with garden crops, and there is not a spear of Quack in it. It so happened that at one of the meetings of our Farmers' Club, the question under discussion was, How to kill Quack-grass? It was stated that land near Rochester, worth five hundred dollars an acre, was so overrun with Quack as to be almost worthless for cultivation, and some of the speakers thought it would have to be abandoned. I was innocent enough to get up and tell the method I had just used for killing Quack on my own farm. "As soon as the wheat crop was off," I said, "I plowed the land, and then harrowed it, and rolled it and harrowed it again until it presented quite a respectable appearance on the surface. The Quack, after the autumn rains, began to grow, and I cross-plowed the field with a steel plow. The grass was so thick and matted that the plow did not make very good work, but as the weather still continued dry, we were able to work the surface into good shape by the use of a thirty-two toothed harrow, which was the only kind we then had. (A Smoothing Harrow, with its seventy-two slanting teeth, would have made far better work, with half the labor.) We kept harrowing it and cultivating it as opportunity offered, and about the last of November we plowed the land again, and left it rough for the winter."

As I talked, it was amusing to watch the expression on the faces of the farmers present. They did not seem to know whether to laugh or sneer, but I imagine they thought it would be better to let the Quack retain possession of the land, rather than to spend so much time in plowing and working it. And I then said: "In the following spring we plowed the field again, and then harrowed and cultivated and harrowed and rolled until the land was completely covered with the dry roots of Quack, which we raked together in windrows and heaps, and then set fire to them. Afterwards we plowed the land once more, harrowed and rolled it, and drilled it in with beans." At this point even the intelligent Secretary of the Club, and an able agricultural writer, could not restrain a look of amazement, that any man could be so destitute of all sense of propriety as to recommend any such a system. But after twenty years' experience, I am prepared to say that the plan was a good one. I had a noble crop of beans that summer, and a good crop of wheat afterwards. From that day to this the field has been the best on the farm, and will pay a higher interest on five hundred dollars an acre than it would have paid at that time on fifty dollars.

I do not say that the whole of this result has been brought about by this extraordinary number of plowings used to kill the Quack, but I feel quite certain that this was the starting point and basis of the improvement. One boy may spend his winter evenings with idle companions, and another at home reading a few good books. The one is never heard of afterwards, the other is the President of a University. I do not say that the books he read that winter evening made him the useful and distinguished man he is, but it was the first of a series of steps which led to honor and renown.

I have spent a great deal of labor on this piece of land, but it has paid for itself from the start; and what I have done myself, I urge others to do, even though the wise men may shake their heads.

ABOUT HIGH FARMING.

We have now far better tools for cultivating land than formerly. In fact, our tools are better than our agriculture. And we may rest assured that so soon as we adopt improved methods of farming and gardening, our inventors and manufacturers will furnish all the tools, implements and machines necessary to do the work.

But will it pay to adopt high farming? That depends on what we mean by high farming. High farming, if we confine ourselves to the production of hay, Indian corn, wheat, oats, and other ordinary farm crops, will not pay in this country. And Sir John Bennett Lawes once wrote a paper or gave a lecture before a Farmer's Club in Scotland, in which he demonstrated that high farming was no remedy for the low prices of agricultural products in Great Britain and Ireland. I think, however, he would admit that thorough cultivation and heavy manuring could be profitably used for the production of what we usually term garden products.

Some years ago I was at an agricultural dinner in

England, when the late J. J. Mechi, who had for many years recommended high farming, stated that, notwithstanding the low price of agricultural products, he was at that time picking several acres of peas for the London market, and he found the crop a very profitable one. Dr. Gilbert, one of the ablest agricultural chemists of the world, called out: "But, Mr. Mechi, this is not farming, it is market gardening." Mr. Mechi, though always ready, made no reply. He seemed to think that the argument was unanswerable, and he let the case go by default. But not so the coming generation of farm boys—and I hope of English boys also. What does it matter whether you harvest your peas dry or pick them green? What does it matter whether you raise cabbages, corn or carrots, and other roots, to be fed out on the farm to animals, or to be sold in market to our fellow citizens, who can not grow them for themselves?

The advocates of high farming make a mistake. Neither England nor New England will ever raise all the wheat required by its population. Even the great State of New York, I hope, will not long continue to raise on its own soil all the wheat it annually consumes. Commerce is the feature of the age, and wheat is carried ten thousand miles to market. Cheap bread is what the world wants, and what the world wants, the world will get. Cheap wheat can never be furnished by high farming. It must and will be grown largely on land manured only by nature. There may be places in which wheat can be profitably grown, where many of the constituents of the plant must be applied to the soil, just as there are places where we can profitably use chemical processes for the production of ice. As a rule, however, nature and commerce will furnish ice cheaper than even modern science can manufacture it. We shall have two kinds of farming. One will consist largely in the production of wheat, corn, oats, barley, cotton, sugar and rice. The other, while it will not entirely neglect these great products, will aim to produce crops which can not be kept from year to year, or ordinarily be transported long distances.

The one system of farming will be carried on with little labor, and little or no manure. And what manure is used will be for the purpose of enabling the plant to abstract as much food as possible from the soil. In other words, our wheat growers may use superphosphate, because the application of phosphoric acid may enable the wheat plant to get a larger quantity of potash, nitrogen, and other constituents of plant food from the soil, and thus to produce larger crops. This is the very reverse of high farming, though it is often very profitable farming. The other system of farming is the one which I want our young men to adopt. The change will be gradual, but it will surely come. It will be adopted in England, and also here. It is absurd to suppose that the soil of England, or of the New England or Middle States, can not be profitably cultivated, owing to the low prices at which the cheap land of the West and Northwest, aided by cheap transportation, can furnish our people, and the people of New England, with bread. Let the bread come, and let us provide good Jersey butter to eat with it. The world as a world spends all it can get, and the less it spends for bread the more it can pay for butter and bonnets, and the bonnet-makers will buy our fruit and vegetables.

COMPETITION IN CROPS.

One thing is certain, we can never get high average prices for wheat, or for any other product which can be grown in all parts of the world, and which will keep from year to year. The farmers of America will never realize extravagant profits from any crop, the value of which is determined by the price it will bring in England. Any crop which is entirely consumed at home will be likely to bring a fair price, and very frequently the price will be determined by the cost at which the article can be brought to our markets from Europe. This was so last year in the case of potatoes and cabbages.

Suppose some of my young friends had had a ten-acre field-garden in high condition, filled with potatoes, cabbages, celery and cauliflowers, not to mention other garden crops. In spite of the drouth and the Colorado-beetle, such a field-garden, prepared, enriched and cultivated, as I have recommended, would have produced three hundred bushels of potatoes per acre. The expense of planting, cultivating, hoeing and digging of these would not exceed thirty dollars per acre, while it would have been an easy matter to have sold the crop for from three hundred to four hundred dollars per acre. So with cabbages. It would not have been a difficult matter to grow five thousand good heads of cabbage per acre, which could readily have been sold at ten cents per head. The planting, cultivating, harvesting, burying for the winter and marketing would not cost over one cent per head, thus affording a profit of four hundred and fifty dollars per acre. This is five per cent interest on nine thousand dollars per acre. We can afford to smile at those who sneer at us for plowing our land four or five times to destroy weeds and get it into good shape for starting a good field-garden. Celery and onions would have afforded still higher profits. Even a few acres of turnips would have made no slight addition to our finances. What has been will be. It may be some years before potatoes and cabbages are again imported into the United States from Europe. It is not at all flattering to our vanity that this vast continent, with its rich land, brilliant sunshine and energetic people, should be obliged to send to the high-priced land of Holland for its sauerkraut, or to Scotland for its potatoes. But we need not fear that the products of our field-gardens will not command profitable prices for years to come. Our population is increasing faster than we can get these field-gardens prepared for the production of the choicer kinds of garden products. There is scarcely a village in England or America which is supplied with all the fresh fruits, flowers and vegetables which the people would take, if they were furnished in good condition and at moderate prices.

THE MANURE QUESTION.

As already said, the real difficulty in starting a field-garden is to get enough manure. We must use all we can scrape up on the farm, and buy all we can get from towns and cities and slaughter-houses, at moderate prices. In addition to this we must plow under a few acres of green crops, and supplement them with liberal purchases of superphosphate of lime and other artificial fertilizers. After we get our field-garden fairly started, it will be a comparatively easy matter to maintain and increase its productiveness. I do not mean by this that we can ever dispense with the use of a large amount of manure. We shall never be able to do so. We may make it cheaper than we do now, or we may be able to use artificial fertilizers with great advantage and economy, but the nature of plants does not change. Early cabbages can never be grown early and of fine quality, except on land supplying in available condition an abundant amount of plant food. All we can hope for is to discover how this great store of plant food can be turned to account after we have grown an early crop of cabbages. Our Experimental Stations will, sooner or later, give us valuable information on this point.

At present we know that it is absolutely necessary to make our field-garden soil excessively rich. We can not adopt high farming in the production of corn and wheat, or oats and peas. Four-fifths of our land will be used as it is now, to produce such crops as good tillage will afford, aided by the use of moderate dressings of artificial fertilizers. Wherever profitable we shall increase the use of lime, ashes and plaster, composted it may be with muck from our swamps.

There is nothing new in all this, for farmers are doing the same thing now. They make a little manure, and they apply it first to one field and then to another. The change I wish to make is to apply the manure to one field only, year after year. I want to introduce the highest kind of "high farming" on a small scale and for special crops. I do not care what the crops are. Even tobacco may be grown in this way, but I do not want to have anything to do with the article. There are better crops to grow, and crops which require as much skill and labor and brains, and which will yield larger profits. As a rule, the crops which require the most labor must have the best land and the heaviest manuring. This is preëminently so in this country, where labor is high and ordinary land cheap. At first it will be well to devote the field-garden to crops which require comparatively little labor and manure. Sweet corn is such a crop, and so are tomatoes, potatoes, beans and late cabbages. The latter crop requires good rich land, but it can be grown in ordinary seasons, with little more than good farm management. If you have any fears that the land is not rich enough to produce a good crop of late cabbages of the large varieties, plant such varieties as the Winningstadt about the middle of July.

Melons and cucumbers and squashes can be grown by the use of a little manure in the hill, aided by a tablespoonful of superphosphate.

Onions must have rich land, and it will be well not to go into this crop too extensively the first year, but I would, by all means, sow some in order to get acquainted with the crop. And so of all other crops you ultimately expect to grow. A little experience will soon enable one to grow them successfully.

THE IMPLEMENTS NEEDED.

The expense of starting the field-garden will consist principally in labor, manure, and seeds. The implements required are found on every well-managed farm, with the exception of a very few.

We shall need a good plow, harrow, roller, cultivator, marker, garden line, seed drill, rake, hoe, transplanting dibble, watering can, potato hook, spade, and fork. These are all necessary, but are already on hand. Amongst the implements not so common, but which, in my own case, I should hardly know how to dispense with, are the Acme Harrow, a Smoothing Harrow, the Gang Plow, and a new Revolving Harrow and Smoother, made by an extensive onion grower in Connecticut. The latter is the best new implement I have tried for many years. Like the original Smoothing Harrow, it is a somewhat crude affair, but it contains the elements of an exceedingly useful and valuable machine. I have had three Smoothing Harrows, and each one is better than its predecessor.

STARTING PLANTS IN THE HOUSE OR HOT-BED.

In the absence of a propagating house, much may be done in the way of starting early plants in one's dwelling or hot-bed. The principal impediment commonly experienced is in the difficulty of obtaining, in the spring, the proper kind of soil or compost to put in the boxes or hot-bed. Professional gardeners prepare the soil with great care the previous year, but if winter is about to set in, and you have nothing ready, excellent results may be obtained by placing in the cellar a load or two of any good light sandy loam; the lighter and richer the better. In the spring, before using it, run it through a sieve, so as to remove all stones and lumps and rubbish. If you have it, mix a tablespoonful of superphosphate to each half bushel of soil; then get some peat—moss, or Sphagnum, such as nurserymen use for packing—dry it thoroughly, and sift it fine, and to each peck of soil put two or three quarts of this fine, dry sifted moss; mix carefully, and you will have as good a material for starting fine seeds as I have ever used.

Leaf-mould is a very fair substitute for moss. It contains much plant food, is light and porous, and retains considerable moisture. By leaf-mould, I do not mean muck from the swamp, but the decomposed leaves and sand scraped up in the woods. Leaf-mould, like muck, varies considerably in composition and value. The best is obtained from Beech, Maple and Oak woods. The leaf-mould should be gathered the previous summer and kept in the cellar until wanted. Before using, it should be mixed with equal parts of sand and sifted. For merely starting plants, rich soil is not essential. Seeds will germinate in moss and sand as well as in the richest mould. After the plants are started and begin to grow, a little plant food is necessary, and in this case leaf-mould is better than moss. Equal parts of sods, sand and well-rotted manure made into a compost and worked over, and sifted until it is fine, is a favorite material for potting plants.

Dried muck from the swamps is an exceedingly useful material for the gardener. In many sections of this country it can be obtained at little more than the cost of cutting, drying, and carting it. No gardener ever has too much of it. It has many excellent properties. It will make heavy soil light. It will make dry soil moist. It will make cold soil warm. It is an excellent absorbent of water and gases. It is itself a manure, and can be used to great advantage in our stables, cow-houses and pig-pens, as well as for mixing with manure in our compost heaps. The practical difficulty is in getting the muck dry and keeping it dry. We want a place for storing it, and above all we want to form the habit of getting muck and using it on our farms and gardens. No one doubts its value, but we hardly know how to commence its use. It is, however, a very simple matter. We usually throw up the muck in the summer and let it lie in a heap until winter, when we have plenty of leisure to draw it. Another plan is to throw it up in July, turn it over a few weeks later to facilitate the drying, and early in the fall, before heavy rains set in, draw it to a shed, or cellar, or barn, where it can be kept dry and ready for use at any time. The farmer who has a good supply of dried muck on hand will find it of great use in many of his gardening operations.

The boxes I have used for starting plants are two feet and one half long, twelve inches wide, and three inches deep, made of half-inch stuff. A screw at each end, about an inch from the top on the outermost corners, is wound round by a piece of wire two feet eight inches long, the other end of the wire being twisted round to a screw fastened to the casement of the window, as shown in the illustration (fig. 1). These boxes are placed on the sill of the window. The length of the box, of course, being determined by the width of the window, it can be made wide or narrow according as you have more or less room in the house. There may be windows where you could have them two feet wide without inconvenience; if so the plants will do just as well, and the boxes, of course, will hold twice the number of plants. I have had better success in starting plants in these boxes in the house, than in a hot-bed as ordinarily managed. The plants are in sight all the time, and are less liable to

Fig. 1.—WINDOW-BOX.

be neglected. The children, especially, soon learn to take an interest in these plant-boxes in the house. They require a little assistance in sifting the soil and moss, and putting it in the boxes, and in fastening the boxes in the window-sills. But they can sow the seed and cover it with a little sifted moss themselves. It is very desirable, however, to write the names of the seeds to be sown, with the date of sowing, on some wooden labels to mark the rows where the different seeds and different varieties are sown. If this is neglected much of the interest will be lost.

MAKING THE HOT-BED.

Whether plants are or are not started in boxes in the house, a hot-bed will be found very useful. If possible this should be placed where a hedge, a fence, or building breaks the force of the wind, admitting at the same time the full rays of the sun. A large quantity of manure is not necessary.

The hot-bed should be covered with five or six inches of light, well prepared soil, and moss or leaf-mould, or dryed and sifted muck, or a compost of rotted sods, etc., as previously described. There are two methods of making a hot-bed. One is to stack fermenting manure on the surface, taking care to build it up regularly and solidly, distributing the long and short manure evenly. Add the manure in layers of about six inches, beating each one down with the fork. The pile should be two or two and a half feet high, with square solid sides, and should be two feet wider and longer than the frame of the hot-bed, as the center is hotter than the outside, which is exposed to the cold air. Another method, and one economical of manure, is to dig a pit two feet wider and longer than the frame. The manure is carefully placed in this excavation, being trodden down evenly and solidly. The management of the hot-bed requires some experience, especially in regard to ventilation and the degree of heat needed by different classes of plants. Cabbage, cauliflower, lettuce, radishes and celery require only a moderate degree of heat, while cucumbers, egg-plant and peppers delight in a soil as warm as your hand, and an atmosphere during the day warmer and more moist then the hottest room. Tomatoes and such flower seeds as phlox, petunia, verbena and aster need a warmer soil than the cabbage, but not so hot as the cucumber. Cucumbers and plants requiring the strongest heat should be placed in the center of the bed, while the cabbage should be placed nearer the outside, either on the top or bottom, where they can be more readily cooled off by opening the sash. If the bed is very hot, more water will be required, and the sash will have to be open longer during the day. If the bed is too cold it is well to surround the outside of the frame with warm manure, and at night cover the sash with a straw mat or blankets; and use only water fully up to blood heat. If the plants are drawn up—if they are tall and thin rather than stout and stocky, it is a sign that the plants are either too thick or the bed too warm. They want fresh air and abundance of sunshine.

COLD FRAMES.

A cold frame is simply a frame and sash of a hot-bed without any manure underneath. Cold frames are quite useful for hardening off plants, but it costs very little more to place a foot or two of manure underneath them, and in our climate a little bottom heat is often very desirable. We can harden off the plants sufficiently by taking off the sash in whole or in part. A well sheltered spot in the garden with a warm sunny exposure is not a bad substitute for a cold frame.

INSECTS.

I am not going to write about insects. I will leave that to the professional Entomologist. We need to know the habits of the various insects which injure or destroy our crops. Last winter one of my neighbors, Col. B., during the busy part of my seed business volunteered to help me by answering letters. He was not used to the business and sometimes got out of patience. One man wanted to know how much onion seed to sow per acre? another the proper time to sow mangels? another whether it was necessary to sow celery in the hot-bed? these and many other similar questions the Colonel, with a little prompting on my part, managed to answer to his own satisfaction, and I hope to the satisfaction of my correspondents. But one man wanted to know the best way to kill Cabbage-worms! I was busy at the time and the Colonel thought he would not bother me, and so he wrote somewhat as follows: "*Dear Sir*—The best way to kill Cabbage-worms is to shoot them. Respectfully yours, Joseph Harris, *per* B."

I do not know who my correspondent was, and do not know whether he applied the Colonel's remedy. No one but a military man would have suggested it. The real trouble is to know where to shoot. It is certainly useless to attack in this way the worms themselves, but if the Colonel meant to have a few days sport with a double barrelled shot-gun, in shooting on the wing the white butterflies which lay the eggs that produce the green Cabbage-worm, the remedy might be popular with the boys. Killing the butterflies, or catching them with nets, is the true way to get rid of the Cabbage-worm.

On my own farm I do nothing to check the ravages of the Cabbage-worm except to dust the plants while the dew is on, with a mixture of plaster and superphosphate, say two parts of plaster to one of superphosphate. I am not sure that it lessens the number of worms, but at any rate it stimulates the growth of the plant, especially if you hoe the mixture into the ground around each plant. The only practical remedy I have ever tried is heavy manuring and thorough cultivation, and setting out plants by the thousand, instead of by the hundred.

THE USE OF POISONS.

With melons, cucumbers, and squashes, the Striped-bug is a great pest. We all get angry enough at them to shoot them, but Hellebore and Paris Green are more effective implements of destruction than the rifle and shot-gun. As soon as the plants appear, it is a good plan, while the dew is on these, to dust them with White Hellebore powder. Paris Green is a more powerful remedy, but needs to be applied, while the plants are young, in very small doses. One of my men, this spring, when we were applying Paris Green to the potatoes, took a pailful of the water containing about a teaspoonful of the Paris Green to the gallon, and applied it to the young cucumber and melon vines in his garden. It killed many of the plants, though it had no injurious effect whatever on the potato vines. If Paris Green is used on melons, cucumbers, squash, etc., I would put in a teaspoonful of the poison to ten quarts of water, or say an ordinary pailful, at the same time stirring into the water two tablespoonfuls of White Hellebore powder. I have used this mixture on young vines without injury. I do not think it will kill all the bugs, but at any rate it greatly lessens their numbers and gives the vines a chance to grow. The real point is to apply the poisonous mixture early enough. If you wait until the bugs appear, they will be very apt to seriously injure the vines before you notice them.

As the vines grow larger the leaves become tougher and less succulent, and there is more strength and vitality in the plant. A stronger mixture of Paris Green, therefore, can be used about the time the vines begin to run. So far as my observation goes, the Striped-bug attacks squash and pumpkin vines several days earlier than the Squash-bug. This is fortunate, for the Squash-bug is much more voracious and destructive to squashes than the Striped-bug. Paris Green applied with water, say about a tablespoonful to ten quarts, is as good a remedy as can be used. I would put on a weak mixture of Paris Green and Hellebore, say a teaspoonful of the first and two tablespoonfuls of White Hellebore powder to ten quarts of water, on young squash, cucumber and melon plants. And for squashes, as soon as the Squash-bugs make their appearance, I would put on Paris Green alone at the rate of one tablespoonful to ten quarts of water. We sprinkle the poison mixed with water on the leaves of the plants with a wisp broom, being careful to keep the water in the pail frequently stirred to prevent the heavy poison from settling to the bottom. I think the reason my man lost his cucumber and melon plants was this: he had been applying Paris Green to the potatoes and had some left at the bottom of the pail. The poison had settled to the bottom, and consequently the mixture he applied to the cucumbers and melons was far stronger than that which he used on the potatoes, and much stronger than is necessary.

Dusting cucumber, melon, and squash plants with plaster early in the morning, when the dew is on, has long been resorted to to check the ravages of the Striped-bug. It is undoubtedly a good thing. A little Paris Green, however, either applied in water or mixed with the plaster, is a much more effective application.

For worms and caterpillars of all kinds which feed on the leaves and stalks of plants, such as the Currant-worm, the Army-worm, and Tent-caterpillar on fruit trees, the caterpillar on celery and tomato plants, and the Potato-worms are all easily destroyed with Paris Green. Their great voracity leads to their destruction. It requires but a single particle of the poison, swallowed with the juice of the leaf to finish them.

London Purple may be better than Paris Green, and there may be other poisons better still. But as we have been using the latter for many years for the Potato-bugs, and have become accustomed to it, we had better continue to use it until something very decidedly better is discovered.

White Hellebore is a far less dangerous poison, especially when applied in water, but it is generally sufficiently powerful to kill all kinds of young worms and caterpillars. Worms and caterpillars are much more easily poisoned than their parent bugs or moths. In other words, a weaker mixture of Paris Green will kill the larvæ or worms of the Potato-bug than is required to kill the bugs or beetles themselves. The worms and caterpillars which feed on the succulent leaves, are little more than sacks of sap, and it ought not to require much poison to wither them up. The Striped-bug, the Squash-bug and the Potato-bug or Beetle, when full grown, are not easily poisoned, and a little hand-picking before they lay their eggs on the leaves can be practised with great advantage, not by any means, however, neglecting to use the poison for the destruction of the larvæ, and young bugs.

CARE OF POISONS.

I need hardly say that too much care can not be exercised in the use of poison. It is dangerous business, and I hope and believe that some article will be discovered which will kill insects and worms, but which will not injure man or beast. In the meantime, I would, so far as possible, limit myself to the use of only one or two poisons, say Hellebore and Paris Green, and they should at all times be kept under lock and key, and the pail or other vessels employed in their use, should be locked up and kept for the special purpose only. This is a matter of much importance, not only for our own safety and that of our animals, but for the accomplishment of the object for which we keep the poison. A prompt application is often absolutely essential to its efficacy. We should therefore, at all times, have every thing connected with the use of the poison, not only in readiness, but where we can easily lay our hands upon it.

CULTIVATION OF VEGETABLES IN THE FARM-GARDEN.

ASPARAGUS.

Sow Asparagus seed in rich, mellow soil, early in the spring, in rows about fifteen inches apart, dropping the seed an inch apart in the rows and covering about one inch deep. When the plants come up hoe the ground between the rows, and pull out any weeds that are among the plants and those that cannot be reached with the hoe. Next spring, when the plants are a year old, set them out in the bed where they are to stay for the rest of their lives. The land should be free from stagnant water. It cannot be too rich. But the real secret of success in growing large asparagus is to give the plants plenty of room and to keep out all the weeds.

If you have no asparagus bed, at least a year's time may be saved by purchasing plants or roots. As a rule, those on sale are two years old. If strong and well grown, one-year-old plants are quite as good as those that are older. In fact, I would rather have a good one-year-old plant than a stunted, two-year-old one. It is never desirable to set out plants that are more than two years' old.

The true plan, if you have no asparagus bed, is to buy roots enough to set out a bed this spring, and at the same time sow a few ounces of seed, as above directed, in another part of the garden. A pound of good seed ought to give at least ten thousand plants.

It would be well to sow the seed thicker than I have

recommended, and then thin out the plants wide enough apart to admit the use of the hoe. In raising asparagus plants, we must aim to keep the land clean by the free use of the hoe rather than by hand-weeding.

The advantage of raising your own asparagus roots is very great. If you take pains to sow on rich, mellow land, and to keep the bed scrupulously free from weeds, you will get stronger and better plants at one year old than the average two-year-old roots generally offered for sale. Then again, when you have your own roots, you can let them remain undisturbed in the original bed until you are ready to transplant them.

MAKING AN ASPARAGUS BED.

The old directions for planting an asparagus bed were well calculated to deter any young gardener from making the attempt. I can recollect very well the first asparagus bed I ever planted. The labor and manure must have cost at the rate of a thousand dollars an acre, and after all was done, no better results were obtained than we now secure at one-tenth the expense. In setting out a large asparagus bed for market, I would make the rows not less than four feet apart, and set out the plants in the rows two and a half to three feet apart, or wide enough to admit the use of the horse-hoe both ways. In growing asparagus we not only want a good crop, but to get it early in the season, and of the largest size. The size and earliness, apart from rich, warm, dry soil, depend principally upon the size and vigor of the roots the previous year. A weak root throws up a weak shoot, while a strong root, in which there is a considerable quantity of accumulated nutriment, will throw up a large shoot early in the season.

It is for this reason that thin planting is so desirable. Thin planting with clean culture, on any ordinarily enriched garden soil, will give us far larger and earlier asparagus shoots than can be obtained from the most elaborately made, and most excessively manured bed, the plants in which are too thick.

It is a popular notion that common salt is exceedingly beneficial as a manure for asparagus. I do not know that there is any positive proof of this, but at any rate, the salt will do no harm, even if applied thick enough to kill many of our common weeds. The salt is usually sown broadcast on the asparagus bed early in the spring, say at the rate of ten bushels per acre. It has been recommended to sow salt at the rate of two or three pounds per square yard, or say at the rate of one hundred and twenty bushels per acre. I mention this to show that salt will not injure asparagus.

In setting out asparagus plants we mark off the rows with a common corn-marker three feet and a half or four feet one way and two feet and a half or three feet the other way. Set out a single plant where the lines cross. It is desirable to disentangle and spread out the asparagus roots horizontally in every direction. On light sandy soil the work can be done with the hand, but on heavier soils it is better to remove the soil with a hoe, at the same time working and loosening the soil underneath. This will greatly facilitate the operation of setting out the plants. I do not think it is necessary or advisable to set out the plants as deep as is sometimes recommended. Three or four inches is deep enough. Sometimes a shovelful of manure is spread on the soil above each plant.

POLE BEANS.

The most delicious of all Beans is the Lima. Like all good things, however, it is more work to grow them than common field beans. They have to be provided with something to cling to. Poles, seven or eight feet long, are best for this purpose. Unless you have poles from the woods, a good plan is to get inch-square strips from the saw mill or lumber yard. Such strips are handy in a garden for many purposes. Strips an inch and a quarter square are much stronger and better, but it is not always so easy to get them. I said Lima-beans could not be grown without some trouble, not only have you to provide poles for them, but they are very tender; they came from a warm climate, and do not like a cold soil. In the tropics the Lima-bean is a perennial plant. It does not need to be raised from seed every year, but the same plant grows on year after year, so the books tell us, and I presume it is true; at any rate the Lima-bean here seems as though it would grow the year round if the weather was warm enough, as it is often growing when the frosts of autumn strike it. We must do all we can to make the soil warm in the spring and to push the plants forward rapidly in summer. A light, sandy soil is warmer and drier in the spring than the heavier and stiffer soils, and Lima-beans can be planted earlier on warm sandy land than on the clay. But the best crop of Lima-beans I ever raised, was on a soil about half way between a sand and a clay; and the poorest crop I ever raised was on very light sandy soil.

I am inclined to think the trouble in the latter case was, that the beans were planted too thickly and were not kept as clean as they should have been. You cannot grow a crop of Lima-beans and a crop of weeds on the same land at the same time; and if you have three hills of beans where there should be only two, one hill is a weed. Lima-beans should not be planted until the soil is warm, or the seed will rot in the ground. Here we can rarely plant before the middle of May. We make hills about four feet apart, and plant six or seven good beans in a hill; four plants in a hill are enough, but you know that something may happen to injure or kill some of them, and so it is better to put in more than you really need, and thin out the weaker plants, leaving three or four of the strongest and best in the hill. It is a good plan to set the pole in the hill before planting the beans. If the pole is not put in until the beans are growing, you are apt to disturb the plants. Put the poles in at least a foot deep, so that the wind will not blow them over when covered with vines. We sometimes plant four or five Lima-beans in a flower pot in the house or hot-bed, and when the plants are well started and the soil is warm enough, we set out the plants in the garden, being careful not to disturb the roots any more than we can help. I have had a very early crop of Lima-beans by adopting this plan.

It is a pity that we cannot get a good dwarf variety of Lima-bean. We have a great variety of excellent dwarf or bush beans that are good for eating, pod and all, in the green state, or good for shelling when green, like Lima-beans and peas, or good for cooking when ripe. It is not often, however, that the same variety of bean is equally good for all these purposes. The Lima-bean is generally used for but one thing. You could not eat the green pods, and they are not often cooked when dry and ripe, though I am told they are very good. They are the most delicious of all beans for shelling and cooking when green.

OTHER POLE BEANS.

There are other varieties that are specially adapted for string beans, that is, for eating the pods while green. I do not know that the pole varieties are any better for this purpose than the dwarf or bush kinds. One of the best varieties of pole beans, is the Speckled Cranberry or London Horticultural. It does not usually grow over five or six feet high, and I have known a good crop raised without poles, but this is a slovenly method which ought not to be tolerated in the garden. Another excellent pole bean is the Scarlet Runner. It is a rampant grower and is frequently used as a screen; the flowers are beautiful and the pods, gathered when young, are delicious.

BUSH BEANS.

For string beans the best variety I have yet grown, is the Black Wax or Butter-bean. The Golden Wax is a larger bean and more productive, but I do not think the pods are any better. The Early Valentine is a little earlier than the Wax or Butter-bean, and on this account deserves a place in every garden. The White Kidney is a very valuable bean. It affords very fair string beans, and the pods, which are not wanted for this purpose, can be left on the vines to ripen, when they will prove very acceptable for boiling and baking.

The cultivation of bush beans is a simple matter. In the field where they are to be cultivated with a horse-hoe, they are planted in rows about thirty inches apart, and five or six beans are dropped in a hill, or place, every twelve or fifteen inches in the row. A larger yield probably could be obtained by drilling the beans continuously in the row, say one bean to each inch; but it is a little more work to pull the beans when ripe, and some of our farmers think it is more work to hoe them. In the garden it is not necessary to plant the beans so far apart. In my own garden, I make the rows fifteen inches apart, and drop the beans about an inch apart in the row. The children are very apt to sow them a good deal thicker than this, and I have noticed that the first dish of beans always comes from the children's garden. As a rule, thick seeding favors early maturity; at any rate this is so with peas, beans, and the grain crops, such as wheat, barley, and oats. Of course there is a limit. If you sow too thickly you would not get any crop at all, and in any case the premature ripening is obtained at the expense of the yield. What I mean is, when you get a very early crop it will usually be a small one. I should plant a row of Early Valentine beans quite thickly, say two beans to each inch of row, and then, a week later, sow a few more rows of Black Wax or Golden Wax, three beans to each two inches of row, and then when the ground is thoroughly warm, about the first week in June, sow the main crop not thicker than one bean to each inch of row. The White Kidney may be sown in the same way and about the same time. I need hardly say that the ground must be kept hoed between the rows, and all the weeds pulled out from between the plants. The Black Wax is the best of all the string beans; a good deal depends, however, on obtaining a good succulent growth, and gathering the pods before they become too old and tough. For this reason it is better to plant at two or three different times in succession, and it is also desirable, in order to favor luxuriant growth, to plant on warm, rich, sandy land, and especially to keep it free from weeds.

BEETS.

The best of all Beets is supposed to be the Egyptian Blood Turnip. The Editor of the AMERICAN AGRICULTURIST once said, that no one knew any thing about beets until he had eaten the Egyptian. It certainly is a delicious beet, but like many other good things it can be spoiled by neglect or bad management. It should be grown rapidly and not too thick in the row, and gathered before it becomes too large and tough. The Bassano beet is very early and easily grown. It is larger than the Egyptian, but the flesh is lighter colored, and on this account not so attractive. The flesh is soft, sweet, and well flavored. Its earliness entitles it to a place in every garden.

The Early Blood Turnip is more extensively cultivated in all sections of the United States than any other variety. It is excellent both for summer and winter use. For winter use, however, it should not be sown before the first or second week in June. I have raised an excellent crop sown as late as the middle of July. As a winter beet the Long Smooth Blood Red is the best variety—or perhaps I should say, it is the most popular variety. For my own use I think the Blood Turnip is just as good a winter beet, if sown late, as the Long Smooth Red, but it is not so productive.

The cultivation of beets is by no means difficult; they will do well on a variety of soils. The great point is to make the land rich and mellow. You can grow beets or Mangel Wurzels on much heavier or more clayey land than you can turnips. The only point is to manure heavily and work the soil thoroughly. Recollect, however, it will not do to work such land while it is wet. Remember also, if you let such land remain unplowed or unspaded until it is baked by our hot sun, you will have a tough job on your hands. You must take it when it is neither too wet nor too dry. Such land ought always to be plowed or spaded in the autumn, and again in the spring, as soon as it is dry enough to crumble to pieces. This kind of heavy land is not easily managed, but when got into good shape and properly cultivated, it stands the drouth well and is immensely productive.

For early beets, it is best to select a warm sandy soil, and sow the seed in rows as soon as the frost is out of the ground. A week and two later sow again. I sow mine in rows fifteen inches apart. I say fifteen inches, not because fourteen inches would not be as good, or sixteen inches would not be better, but because I happen to have a garden marker that makes rows fifteen inches apart, a distance which suits most crops. It costs no more to hoe a row fourteen or fifteen inches wide than one which is only seven or eight inches wide. The boys who cultivate corn, going twice in a row, will understand why this is so. If your corn is three and a half feet apart, is is no more work to cultivate it than if it was two and a half or three feet apart, for the simple reason that you and the horse have to go up and down each row, no matter how wide or how narrow it may be, and so it is with hoeing. If the hoe, when placed by the side of the plants in the drill, will reach the center of the row, it is no more work to hoe a wide row than a narrow one. And there are many reasons in favor of wide rows, especially in our dry, hot climate. Vegetables and garden crops of nearly all kinds need dry, rich land, and an abundance of moisture. The dry land we get by underdraining where needed. The rich land we get by heavy manuring, and the moisture we get by killing weeds and keeping our cultivated plants a good distance apart. Plants evaporate large quantities of water, and if you have three plants on a spot of land containing only moisture enough for two, the growth of these three plants will be checked for want of the necessary moisture. As a rule we can not profitably increase the supply of water, but we can very easily reduce the number of plants.

Sow the beets in rows fifteen inches apart, and thin out the plants in the rows to four or five inches apart; then, as the plants grow, thin them out still more, as soon as any of them are large enough to use, and you will have an abundant supply of this healthful and delicious vegetable.

In good beet seed there are two or three seeds together in a sort of very rough bur. If the seed is sown with a drill it is necessary to recollect that seed varies greatly in size. American-grown seed is much larger than that which is imported. And Egyptian Blood Turnip is nearly always a small inferior looking seed.

Our garden drills have a hole for sowing beet seed, but this hole would either sow the Egyptian too thick or the Bassano, or Dewing's Blood Turnip, or the Long Smooth Red much too thin. If the seed is good, it is not necessary to drop more than one seed to every inch of row. Of course it is not necessary to sow even so thick as this, but it is better and safer to sow three or four times more than you need, rather than to run the risk of having the crops too thin.

MANGEL WURZEL.

Mangel Wurzels are simply large beets grown for cattle, sheep, and swine. Any one who can raise beets in the garden can raise Mangel Wurzels in the field. All there is to be done is to make the land as rich in the field and keep it as clean and mellow as you do in the garden. It would be a good thing, however, to sow a few Mangel Wurzels in the garden until you became familiar with its habit of growth. I once had a farmer's son hoeing Mangels for me in the field, and I had the greatest difficulty in persuading him to thin them out sufficiently. The plants were very small and he wanted to leave them about an inch apart in the row, while I wanted him to leave only a single good plant to every foot of the row. The land was rich and we had moist, growing weather, and in less than a month the plants, though a foot apart in the row, completely covered the ground. "I had no idea that such little bits of things could grow so rapidly," he said. Had his father encouraged him to sow a few Mangel Wurzels in the garden he would have known better.

If you sow Mangel Wurzels in the garden, mark off the rows fifteen inches apart, and then run the same marker across the rows and drop three or four seeds, where the lines cross, and cover them about an inch deep, patting the ground smooth with the back of the hoe, just as you do when planting corn in the field. When the Mangel Wurzels are fairly up, hoe them and thin out the plants, leaving only one good strong plant in each hill. Suffer not a weed to grow, and if the land is rich enough you will have a great crop of roots. Next year you may wish to plant an acre or two in the field.

There are several varieties of Mangel Wurzel; in color they are nearly all either red or yellow. The red, however, is not by any means a deep bright red like the Blood Turnip, or the Long Smooth Blood Beet. There is no mistaking the one for the other.

In shape we have round, or globe Mangels, and the long varieties, with an intermediate class, called ovoids.

This gives us six distinct kinds of Mangel Wurzel, and in addition to these six, we have a great number of varieties, or at any rate a great number of names. We have Carter's Yellow Globe, and Sutton's Yellow Globe, and Harris' Yellow Globe. All that is meant by it, or at any rate all I mean by it is, that we have taken great pains to select every year just such Mangels as come nearest to our idea of what a good root should be, and we set out these roots for seed. They are not distinct varieties, but merely good strains which we wish to propagate.

It would be a good thing for a farmer's son to get into the habit of selecting some of the best Mangels and setting them out for seed. I am not going to tell you which is the best variety of Mangel or the best strain to grow. On my own farm we prefer the Yellow Globe.

They do not grow so deep in the ground as the long kinds, and are much more easily harvested. We think they are not so coarse as the Long Red Mangel, and we have a fancy that the yellow Mangel makes yellower butter than the red. Probably this is nothing but fancy.

I have weighed a big crop of Long Red and Yellow Globe Mangel, growing side by side in the same field, and the scales indicated very little difference in the two crops. The general impression, however, is that the Long Red will produce a larger crop per acre than the Ovoid or Globe varieties.

THE CABBAGES.

The Cabbage is well worth studying. Some people have got in the habit of sneering at cabbage growers. It is a fact, that a man who cannot read or write will sometimes beat the best of us in growing cabbages. His success, however, is not due to his ignorance. You will find he has thoroughly studied the wants of the vegetable. If he knows nothing else he knows how to grow cabbages.

Cabbages require preëminently rich land. It must be preternaturally rich. People say that land which will produce corn will produce cabbages. I doubt it. Land may be rich enough for a good crop of corn that is not rich enough to produce even a fair crop of cabbages. The reason of this probability is, that corn is a natural crop, while the cabbage is an artificial production. We do not raise cabbages for seed as we do corn. We raise it for the heads or tender leaves or sprouts. Naturally it runs up to seed the first year, but this is not what we want. We want a cabbage that will grow rapidly and produce a large mass of leaves good for food. For this purpose we require a well-trained, or cultivated variety, having this artificial character thoroughly established. We also want, and must have, very rich land.

Early cabbages require richer land than the late varieties. But you can grow twice as many plants on an acre. I know one gentleman who makes a great deal of money from his crop of early cabbages. He plants about three acres every year, some of it on land which had been in other crops the previous year, and some of it on land which has grown cabbages for several years. His crop on the old land is earlier and better than that on the new soil. No matter how heavily he manures the new land, he cannot make it as productive the first year as the old piece; the reason is, that the manure can not be so thoroughly worked into the soil the first year. This is a point of great importance in horticulture. We not only need to manure our land heavily, but to thoroughly mix the manure with the soil.

EARLY CABBAGE PLANTS.

Early cabbages bring a high price, and it will pay to take extra pains with them. There are two ways of raising early cabbages, one is by setting out plants which were started the autumn previous and wintered over in cold frames. The other plan is by sowing the seed in a hot-bed or greenhouse early in the spring, and when the plants are large enough and have been properly hardened off, set them out in the field or garden. It is possible to get the cabbages just as early from the spring-sown plants as from those sown in autumn. As to which is best depends very much on circumstances. Recent practice seems to be tending more and more toward the use of spring-sown plants.

Where only a few plants are needed for home use, a good plan is to sow a little seed in a box in the house. After the plants are up you must give them as much sun as possible, and be careful not to keep them in too warm a room. During warm days the box may be placed out of doors in the sun, in a spot sheltered from the prevailing wind. Cabbages are hardy, and when raised in a hot-bed or in the house they are much more likely to be kept too warm than too cool. The great point is to give them plenty of sun and plenty of room; if they are too thick in the box they must be transplanted or pricked out into another box. The oftener they are transplanted, and the more room you give them, the stronger and healthier they become. It is very desirable to have strong, stocky plants. As soon as the land is dry enough to work properly, and the plants are large enough and strong enough to set out, prepare the land by spading or plowing, and harrow or rake until it is fine and mellow. Then set your line and mark out the land in rows two and a half feet apart, and with a dibble set the plants twenty inches to two feet apart in the row.

The best and earliest variety for market is the true Jersey Wakefield, but for home use the Early York is still preferred by many. In Western New York we get the Jersey Wakefield large enough for market about the first of July—sometimes a little earlier, and sometimes a little later, according to the season.

SECOND EARLY CABBAGES.

For second early cabbage we have several excellent varieties. Henderson's Summer is a favorite variety with market gardeners. It makes a large head and looks very attractive. So far as my experience goes, however, it is not of the highest quality, and for my own use I should prefer Winningstadt, or Fottler's Drumhead.

The method of cultivation of these second early cabbages is the same as for the early, except that the land need not be quite so rich, and the plants should be set a little farther apart. For late summer or early autumn cabbages it is not necessary to raise the plants in a hot-bed. Sow the seeds in a warm, sheltered spot in the garden, as soon as the ground can be got into good condition. Drill in the seed in rows fifteen inches apart, and drop about four seeds to each inch of row. We generally sow a little thicker than this in hopes that the plants will have a better chance of escaping the ravages of the little black beetle which is almost certain to attack them. Frequent hoeing is particularly desirable, as it not only kills weeds and favors the growth of the plants, but it has a tendency to frighten away the black beetle. For late autumn or winter cabbages we sow our cabbage seed from the middle of May until the first week in June. The larger and later the variety the earlier should the seed be sown. The summer and early autumn varieties, such as the Winningstadt, Henderson's Summer, Fottler's, Stone Mason, and Harris' Short Stem Drumhead can be changed into winter cabbages by sowing the seed from the last week in May until the first week in June. I have had a good crop of most of these varieties when the plants were set out as late as the middle of June; as a rule, however, it is better to plant earlier.

On my own farm, where we raise cabbage plants in very large quantities, we drill the seed in rows twenty-one inches apart, and keep the crop clean by the frequent use of the horse-hoe. You need the cleanest, richest and best land, and in addition to this, sow four hundred pounds of superphosphate per acre. With good clean land, a dressing of superphosphate and the frequent use of the horse-hoe between the rows, it is a very easy matter to raise cabbage plants. You can grow from one hundred and fifty thousand to two hundred thousand good cabbage plants to the acre. When much thicker than this, the plants are not so stocky as they should be. The price paid for good cabbage plants is from two dollars to three dollars per thousand.

LATE CABBAGES.

For the main crop of winter cabbages, the large late Flat Dutch or Premium Flat Dutch, or, if the land is rich enough, the Mammoth Marblehead are all excellent varieties. I have said that late cabbages do not require such rich land as the early. This is true, and yet it seems to be a fact that when you sow the early varieties late in the season, for the purpose of using them for a late fall or winter crop, these smaller and earlier varieties will do better on moderately rich or comparatively poor soil,

Fig. 2.—SAVOY CABBAGE.

than the larger and later varieties. I know some experienced cabbage growers who raise the Winningstadt for the main crop, because they find that it is sure to head, while, from want of plenty of manure, they can not grow the larger and later varieties. When late cabbages are raised as a field crop, a good plan is, to mark out the land three feet apart each way, and set out a plant where the lines cross. This gives four thousand eight hundred and forty plants to the acre. The advantage of the plan is, that you can cultivate the ground both ways between the plants with a horse-hoe, and the labor of tending the crop is very slight.

SAVOY CABBAGES.

The Savoy Cabbages are so unlike ordinary cabbages that some works place them under a separate head, as Savoys. In the Savoys the leaves are strongly wrinkled, or blistered, and the heads are never very solid. In texture and flavor they are more like a cauliflower than like the ordinary winter cabbages, being very tender and marrow-like, and most delicious to those who like cabbages at all. They are among the hardiest of cabbages, and may be left out until the last. Their cultivation is the same as that of other late varieties.

THE CAULIFLOWER.

The cultivation of the Cauliflower is very similar to that required for the cabbage. The method of raising the plants is the same; the time and manner of setting out is the same; the distance apart is the same, as is the method of preparing and enriching the land. The only difference is, that the cauliflower, being a little more delicate, every operation must be conducted with greater care and thoroughness. The profits of the crop are very large, and it will pay those who raise it to spare no pains that will insure success.

There was a time when it was thought that the American climate was particularly unsuited to the growth of the cauliflower; such, however, is not the case. We are now satisfied that as good cauliflowers can be grown here as in any other country. Our hot sun, which was supposed to render the cultivation difficult, if not impossible, is, in point of fact, a great advantage; but we must make other things correspond. If the soil is dry, poor, hard, cloddy and weedy, the hot sun may be an injury; it will wither up the cauliflowers and the careless cultivator will be very apt to blame the sun. But if your land is well drained, moist, rich, mellow, deeply and thoroughly cultivated and free from weeds; if you have good strong cauliflower plants of the right variety, and set out at the right time; if the roots have got firm hold of the soil and have access to abundance of food and water, let the sun shine, the leaves of the plant will glory in the abundant sun; and if they wilt a little during the fierce heat of the day, the next morning will find them bright and fresh and full of vigor.

I would advise no one to go extensively into the cultivation of cauliflowers before they have had some experience; better raise a few in the garden and make special efforts to grow them to perfection. When you have learned the secret of success, extend their cultivation to the field and market garden. The standard varieties of cauliflower are Early Paris, Erfurt Earliest Dwarf, Large Lenormand and Walcheren. The former two are early varieties, and the last two are larger and later. What we have said in regard to the planting of early and late varieties of cabbage, is equally true in regard to the planting of early and late varieties of cauliflower. To have early cauliflowers, of course, you must sow early varieties, but for a late crop, it is not absolutely necessary to have late varieties. If late kinds are planted early and every thing goes well, they will give you a larger, handsomer, and more profitable crop; but it often happens, where the soil and season are not propitious, that the early varieties planted late will give the best results. In other words, if you can grow a large crop of the late varieties do so. But if you have any reason to anticipate a failure, you had better be content with raising a crop of the early and smaller varieties planted late. You can sometimes grow a good crop of Early Paris or Erfurt Earliest Dwarf, when you can not get a single head of Large Lenormand or Walcheren.

Except for the earliest crop, it is not necessary to raise the plants in a hot-bed. Sow, out of doors, on the richest, warmest, and mellowest soil you have, in rows fifteen inches apart, as directed for cabbage seed. The late varieties should be sown just as early as the ground is in good working condition. The early varieties, when intended for a late crop, need not be sown before the middle of May, and they will often do well if not sown until the first of June. Keep the plants well hoed. If too thick, prick them out into a border of rich, moist land, in rows a foot apart, and at two or three inches distant in the row. Let them stay there until wanted, they will make fine, strong, stocky plants, and well repay you for the extra labor of pricking out.

CARROTS.

The Carrot is not a popular crop. Horses are very fond of carrots, but then they never had to weed them. If they had been obliged to get on their hands and knees, so to speak, with the hot sun on their backs, and had to weed and thin carrots, when Tom and Dick were gone a fishing, they would have been satisfied with dry corn and hay. Boys ought to know better. If we want a good thing, we have got to work for it. The horse, I have no doubt, would go without the carrots rather than perform the necessary work of raising them. But we want horses to work for our pleasure, and a good horse that behaves himself, and does cheerfully all that we ask of him, is entitled to an occasional feed of fresh juicy carrots to mix with his dry hay and corn. But I am sure our bright American boys will soon learn to make the horse do nine-tenths of the work of raising the carrots. Just think of it! When I was a boy, we used to make a bed about five feet wide, trim it off at the edges with a sharp spade, throw the soil on top from the alleys, rake the bed, and then sow the carrot seed broadcast, and make the bed smooth by patting it with the back of the spade. These beds of carrots, onions, etc., looked very neat and trim when first made, but oh! the labor of weeding them! By and by we made a wonderful discovery, we found that carrots, onions, etc., could be sown in rows two or three inches apart, where we could dig up the weeds with a knife or our fingers. Gradually the rows were made wider apart, and now almost every one drills in his carrots, onions, parsnips, etc., in rows wide enough apart, to admit the use of a good American hoe.

IMPROVED CARROT GROWING.

I want to do still better. I want the horse to do all of the hoeing. I sow my carrots in rows twenty-one inches apart, and cultivate them with a horse-hoe. If you have a steady horse and a good cultivator, and will give your mind to the work, you can run very close to the rows, and leave very little to be done in the way of hand-weeding or hoeing. In fact, if you will run the cultivator between the rows once a week after the plants get fairly started, they will grow so rapidly that they will smother out or hold in check nearly all the weeds. I tell my boys that cultivating between such narrow rows is an education. It is good mental discipline, for they must keep their mind constantly fixed on their work.

Much of the success of the plan, however, will depend upon having the land not only rich, but in the best mechanical condition. Fortunately our inventors and manufacturers are fully abreast of the times. We have a good gang-plow, with bright steel mould-boards, that will turn over three furrows at a time, and leave the land almost smooth and level. Then we have a harrow that will cut the clods to pieces, and still further smooth and mellow the land. After that, we make use of a smoothing harrow. This, with a roller passed over the land two or three times, first the harrow and then the roller, I formerly thought left the land in as good shape as we could hope to get it by the use of horse-implements, and that anything further in the way of fining or smoothing the surface soil must be done with a steel rake. But no, we have now a revolving harrow and leveler, that will leave the land as smooth and fine as it can be made with a steel rake, at one-tenth of the expense. With these implements, a garden line, a marker, and a good drill, field-gardening is a much more pleasant and profitable business than ever before in the history of the world.

There is one thing which our drill makers need to do, which is to give us a bright, steel coulter for depositing the seed in the row. The various seed drills have rough cast-iron coulters two inches wide, and are admirably adapted for doing poor work. The coulter catches every bit of straw, or root, or grass, or rubbish it comes in contact with. The seeds are scattered in a wide row. Instead of this we want a narrow, bright steel coulter that would run easily and smoothly through the soil, and deposit the seed in a row not over a quarter of an inch wide. It would not only do better work, especially when the land was damp and sticky, but as can be readily seen, these narrow drills would leave very much less space for hand weeding. In fact a skillful boy, with the right kind of hoe, could run so close to this narrow row that he would not leave one weed in a thousand that would have to be pulled out with the fingers. Another thing in regard to the culture of carrots which I think is important: you know the time was, when onion growers thought it was necessary to thin out the onions, leaving only one plant every three or four inches; but we have discovered that the onion will bear crowding. If three or four onions be left in a bunch, they will push each other upwards and downwards, lengthwise and sidewise, and you will get three or four good sized onions instead of one large overgrown one which no one wants. And so it is with carrots. Such varieties as the Early Short Horn or the Half Long will bear a good deal of crowding. I have often left four or five carrots in a bunch and had them all grow to good size. They push each other sidewise in the loose, well cultivated soil. Leaving them thick in this way not only saves the unpleasant labor of thinning with the fingers, but this thick crop of carrots keeps down the weeds in the row and saves much labor in weeding.

The true plan is, to sow the carrots pretty thick, dropping, say two or three seeds to each inch of row, and instead of thinning them out by hand, as is usually done, I would push or pull a narrow hoe through them and thus leave a bunch of plants every five or six inches in the row; each bunch may have four or five carrots, which will grow strong enough to keep down the weeds which may be left in the bunch, and the entire work of weeding can be done with a cultivator and hoe. The large long varieties of carrots, like the Long Orange and White Belgian, can not be left so thick in the bunches, and for this reason, I prefer to grow the Half Long variety; it is more nutritious and is much more easily harvested.

CELERY.

Celery is a crop which should be largely grown in the field-garden. It is essentially a farm crop, just as much so as cabbage. I mean by this that it requires a good deal of space, and should be grown on the farm where land is comparatively cheap, rather than in suburban market gardens, where land is worth from five hundred dollars to five thousand dollars an acre. Vegetables which must be marketed fresh every morning, must be grown near the market, but this is not necessarily the case with Celery.

When I was a boy it was quite an affair to grow celery. We dug trenches and heavily manured the bottom, put three or four inches of soil on top of the manure, and set a single row of plants six or eight inches apart in the row. The work was done with a spade, and celery was a costly luxury. Where land was high, we sometimes, instead of planting a single row, made the trench four or five feet wide, covered the bottom with manure, put on the soil, and planted four or five rows eight or ten inches apart in this wide trench. I have seen a good crop raised in this way, but it is a great deal of work and will not pay. The truth is, that celery requires a great deal of moisture; it needs rich land too, but moisture will, to a certain extent, take the place of manure. If you can get land that is well drained and moist also, that is the true place for celery. If the land is not moist you must set the plants farther apart in the rows. For early celery, of which comparatively little is required either for home use or market, the seed must be sown in a hot-bed or in a box in the house. You can sow the seed in rows one inch apart and ten or twelve seeds to each inch of row. When the plants begin to crowd one another, dig them up and prick them out into a cold-frame or cooler hot-bed, or into a larger box in the house. In two or three weeks they will probably need to be transplanted again into a cold-frame or warm border out of doors; set them in rows wide enough apart to admit the use of a hoe, keep clean, and let them remain until wanted to set out.

For the main crop, the seed should be sown in a warm sheltered spot as early in the spring as the soil is in good working condition. The better plan is to prepare the ground the previous autumn, and the more manure you can work into it, the better. Do this as early in the fall as the land can be spared; this will give the weed seeds in the manure and in the soil a chance to germinate. Work the ground several times, for the more you work it, the more weed seeds will germinate and be destroyed; this is very important, because celery seed is slow to germinate in the cold soil in the spring, and if the land is full of weed seeds, they will start long before the seeds of the celery and cause a great deal of trouble in hoeing and weeding. It is folly to endeavor to raise celery plants unless the land is very rich, and is kept scrupulously clean. If the land has been carefully prepared in the autumn, I would not plow or spade it in the spring, as that would bring up the cold soil to the surface. As soon as the frost is out of the first three or four inches of the surface soil, hoe the bed and rake it with a steel rake, and make it fine and smooth. Then mark rows ten inches apart, and sow the celery seed evenly in the rows, depositing ten or twelve seeds to each inch of row, with a radish seed every three or four inches apart in the row. The radish seed will germinate quickly, and show you where the rows are, and enable you to hoe lightly between them, long before the celery makes its appearance. The great point is, to get strong, stocky plants with an abundance of fine roots. For this purpose it will be necessary, not only to keep the bed very clean, but to thin out the plants where too thick. The plants ought to be not less than an inch to two inches apart in the row. When ready to transplant, the bed should be saturated with water, and the right way to do this, is to take a fork or spade and thrust it down deep into the soil between the rows and below the roots of the celery, and lifting up or breaking up in such a way as to leave the bed full of cracks and holes. In this manner you can get several barrels of water upon, or rather into, a small bed. The next morning, if the bed has been thoroughly saturated, the plants can be taken up with all their roots, and more or less fine soil still adhering to them.

In raising celery plants on a large scale, I find it desirable to sow the seed in rows twenty-one inches apart, or far enough to admit the use of a horse-hoe. This not only saves much labor in hoeing, but the frequent use of the horse-hoe keeps the land loose and mellow, and when you wish to set out the plants, they can be taken up much more easily and with a large mass of fine roots, with soil adhering to them. Before commencing to fork up the plants, we run a narrow cultivator several times between the rows as deep as we can get it; set out the plants with as little exposure of the roots to the air as possible. It does not hurt a plant to wilt when the wilting is caused merely by the evaporation of water through the leaves, but it is a serious injury to let the roots shrivel up from exposure to our hot sun and drying winds.

SETTING OUT THE PLANTS.

Before transplanting, however, it is necessary to get trenches ready. In point of fact, the trenches are not trenches at all, according to the old meaning of the term. The way I have done the work on my own farm is to get the land ready by plowing and harrowing until it is quite smooth and mellow. I then take a marker with teeth four feet apart, set a line for the first row and run the marker along the line. After the land is all marked out into rows four feet apart, take a double mould-board plow, with two horses, and run the plow along the row made by the marker. If you have not a double mould-board plow, the work can be done equally well with an ordinary plow; except that it is necessary to go twice in a row, up and down, instead of once. You will see that this is simply making what are called dead furrows, every four feet.

When the work is done, draw out some of the richest, most thoroughly rotted manure you can find and spread in the rows, or dead-furrows. Spread it evenly and knock it to pieces thoroughly with a hoe or potato hook, mixing more or less soil with it, getting it, at any rate, well broken to pieces. Then with a plow throw the soil back again into the furrow; then roll and harrow and roll again, until you have made the soil as fine as possible. Then take your four-foot marker again, set the line exactly where it was in the first place, and run the marker along the line just over where the manure has been put. If the work has been well done, you will have five or six inches of good mellow soil in which to set out your celery plants. I set my plants a foot apart in the row; as the rows are four feet apart we get ten thousand eight hundred and ninety plants to the acre.

Of course plants can be grown much closer than this. The rows can be made three feet apart and the plants set six inches apart in the row. This would give twenty-nine thousand and forty plants to the acre, and if the land is rich enough, moist enough and clean enough, and you have the best plants, and give them the best of treatment, and the season is every way favorable, you can get just as good celery from the thicker planting as from the thin. But my land is simply ordinary farm land and an acre or two more or less, provided it will save labor, and insure a crop in an unfavorable as well as a favorable season, does not count. Certainly I would advise any farm boy, whose father will furnish the land rent free, for a given number of celery plants, not to make the rows too near, or set out the plants too close in the rows.

Some of the old market gardeners may criticise me for

recommending such thin planting, but I know what I know. I know that their land, which has been in garden culture for many years, is in a very different condition from our very best farm land, and it will be far better the first year or two, when trying to raise garden crops on farm land, not to plant too thickly.

In setting out the celery plants, select damp weather if possible, but a damp or rainy day is not half so necessary as a finely worked, mellow and moist soil. If the ground is dry and cloddy, so that the dry lumps of earth will tumble into the hole made by the dibble, you had better let the plants stay where they are, and go to work with a roller and harrow until you have made the soil fine and mellow. I know that this can be done, and it is sometimes necessary to go over the land half a dozen times or more with a roller and harrow. I put one team to the roller, and a three-horse team to a Smoothing Harrow. Having the boy ride on the harrow so as to press it into the soil, let him go ahead and stir up the soil, bringing the lumps to the surface. The roller follows and crushes the surface; then go over it again, going round and round the lumpy piece until every lump is broken up fine. Even a very light shower will make such a well-worked soil moist enough to allow the plants to be set out, and if we do not have any shower, the moisture will in time come up from the subsoil and make the ground moist enough to insure the safety of the plants. A recently transplanted row of celery often presents a sorry appearance in our dry climate. But do not be discouraged. If the roots and the crowns of the plants are alive they will in time start into growth. If the plants were set out during a rain, and the surface of the soil afterwards bakes or becomes hard, the crust should be broken up fine with a hoe. An inch or two of dry, loose earth on the surface checks evaporation and keeps the soil moist underneath where the roots are. Always remember this, as it is very important. A dry surface, if the soil is loose and fine, is a good thing, provided there is sufficient moisture in the soil below, around the roots.

As the celery grows, keep the ground well cultivated and hoed; and this is all that need be done until the plants have nearly attained their growth. The earth is then drawn round the plants in order to blanch the stalks. You will soon learn how to do this. It is necessary to gather up the loose and straggling stalks, and press the whole plant firmly together with the hand in order to prevent the soil falling into the center or "heart" of the plant between the stalks. Draw the soil around the plant, fully up to the lower leaves, and if the weather is fine and the plants continue to grow, earth them up again.

STORING FOR WINTER.

There are several plans for keeping celery during the winter. My own method is to dig a trench in dry, sandy land, a foot wide, and deep enough to hold the plants. In this set the plants upright, just as they grew, only putting them close together crosswise of the trench. The more soil there is left adhering to the roots the better. It is also desirable and certainly much more pleasant, to do the work when the soil and plants are dry. But as we wish to let the celery keep on growing as long as the weather will allow, it is not always that we can find a pleasant day so late in the season in which to secure our celery crop. We have to do the best we can. As before said, it is desirable to put up the plants when dry, but if the work is not done until just before winter is about to set in, there is not much danger that the celery will mould, no matter how wet it is when put in the trench.

My plan is, to plow the earth away from the rows of

celery in the field; for this we use a plow from which the mould-board is removed, leaving only the point and the land-side. By running this plow on the side of the row, with the point below the roots, the soil is made so loose that the plants can be pulled with great ease and rapidity. We drive a stone-boat along the side of the row, and place the plants upon this, and take them to the trench where they are to be placed for the winter. The stalks and leaves are straightened out, and the plants are placed as thickly as they will stand in the trench, and it will not in the least hurt the celery if there is a little fine earth put between each layer of plants. I place a strip of corn stalks or straight straw lengthwise along the sides of the trench and draw the soil up to it. We then plow two or three furrows on each side of the trench, if necessary going round and round the trench two or three times, until the soil on each side is broken up very loose and fine to the depth of eighteen or twenty inches, and three or four feet wide. Such a loose mellow soil will stand the severest zero weather with little or no freezing. And if a few leaves are plowed into the soil or placed on top of the trench, there is no danger that the celery will be injured by the frost. If the work is well done, there will be little danger of the rain getting into the trench; but to avoid all risk, we sometimes place a board lengthwise of the trench, on top of the celery, and cover it with leaves or straw, with three or four inches of straw on top. The plowing round and round the trench several times, until the ground is made very mellow and deep, I regard as very essential, for it enables you to get out the celery at any time when it is wanted during the winter.

Another plan for preserving celery for winter use, is to put it in a box in the cellar with layers of earth between the plants, placing the celery in the box upright in the same way we recommended placing it in the trench out doors. Another method recommended by Mr. Henderson in the AMERICAN AGRICULTURIST is, to set up boards on edge in the cellar, nine inches wide and as high as the plants are tall. A few inches of soil being placed at the bottom, the celery is set in this board trench the same as in that in the ground. At nine inches from the first, other boards are set up in the same manner, and so on.

In regard to varieties, I have had the best success with the Dwarf White and the Dwarf Crimson. The Boston Market has a more spreading habit and throws up numerous side shoots or suckers, which, when well grown and blanched, are very crisp and toothsome. There are those who still prefer the larger varieties known by different names, such as Giant, Superb, Leviathan, etc. Unquestionably in this climate the dwarf varieties, as a rule, are more easily grown and more likely to give satisfaction.

CELERIAC, OR TURNIP-ROOTED CELERY.

Celeriac is a variety of celery, but much hardier, and having a less erect growth, the plants forming a bulbous enlargement; hence the name Turnip-Rooted. Its cultivation is extending in this country, and when well grown it is certainly a delicious vegetable. We have hardly yet learned how to grow it to perfection. The cultivation is in many respects similar to that required for celery, but it is not necessary to have the rows so far apart, as no earthing up is required. Set out the plants in rows thirty inches apart, and a foot apart in the row. The land can not be too rich or mellow, or the cultivation too thorough. The plants are inclined to throw up suckers. These should be removed as soon as they start; otherwise these suckers will check the tendency of the plant to form a bulb. This is perhaps the most important point to be observed in the culture of celeriac. It would not be desirable to go into the cultivation of celeriac on a large scale until one has had some experience,

Fig. 3.—CELERIAC.

but it is a crop which it would be well for every one to raise on a small scale until he gets acquainted with its merits and uses.

CORN—SWEET-CORN.

Corn is so easy to grow that very few grow it to perfection. Seedsmen get more scoldings with reference to their corn than about any other seed. Every one thinks he can grow it, and when the crop fails, we naturally blame the person who sells us the seed. One year I had a very choice variety of corn and distributed it freely among my friends, but many wrote me that not a kernel of it grew. I never felt quite sure whether they did not know how to plant the corn, or whether I did not know how to save the seed. The truth is, if you get a very choice variety of tender, sweet and delicious corn to be eaten green, it is a very difficult matter to preserve the seed without weakening its germinative power; and even if the seed is as good as we can hope to get it, sweet corn, if is is really sweet and good, can not safely be planted in as cold and damp a soil as common field corn. We all wish to get sweet corn as early as possible, and it is worth while running the risk of losing our first planting, in order to occasionally secure a few dishes of very early corn. It is simply the loss of a little seed, for if it fails to grow, owing to the soil being too cold and damp, or to the crop being destroyed by an early frost, the soil can afterward be replanted with a later variety of corn, or used for some other crop. But do not wait until your first planting is lost before planting again. Plant a few hills as soon as the ground can be got into good working condition, and a few days later, especially if the weather is warm and dry, plant a few more hills, and a few days later still put in a larger quantity; in this way, three years out of four, you will be pretty certain to secure a good supply of this most delicious and popular American vegetable.

The land for sweet corn should be prepared in the autumn, and the surface soil, especially, should be heavily manured. In the fall get the soil all ready for planting, and in the spring do not plow or spade the land, but make a few hills by drawing the surface soil together with a hoe. For early corn in the garden, and with dwarfish varieties, like the Early Minnesota, the rows need not be more than three feet apart, or the hills more than eighteen or twenty inches apart in the row. Use seed freely, for in the cold, damp soil, much of it may fail to grow. I would plant eight or ten kernels in each hill, and if they all grow, pinch off (not pull up,) all but four of the best plants. If you undertake to pull up the plants you will be apt to disturb or injure those which are left in the hill. As the plants grow, draw a little fresh earth up to them, and if you have reason to fear a frost some night, it is worth while to take pieces of newspaper, say a foot square, and lay them over the hills of corn, putting a little soil on each corner to hold them down. The next morning they can be turned back and still kept by the side of the hill, weighted with a little earth, ready for use the next night if necessary. It requires but a very slight covering to protect plants from frost, but it will not do to let the covering remain on all the time, as they need exposure to the sun.

VARIETIES.

The later varieties of corn, such as Crosby's Sugar, Russell's Prolific, and Moore's Early Concord, though far sweeter and better, do not need so much care as we have recommended when we wish to secure the earliest possible dish of corn. But even for the second early crop, it will pay to take pains in the preparation of the soil, planting, and cultivation. You can not grow good sweet corn as easily as you can good field corn. For the main crop, Stowell's Evergreen is one of the most popular varieties; as ordinarily grown, however, it has ceased to be evergreen, it is simply a good late variety of sweet corn. It is the variety generally grown for the canning and evaporating establishments, and the growers for these are particularly anxious to get a strain of Stowell's Evergreen corn, which has ceased to be evergreen, and which is sure to mature in a good season. Those who wish so-called "Evergreen" corn, must get seed of this variety which has been grown several degrees farther south than where it is intended to plant it.

The canning establishments engage farmers to raise sweet corn for them. They furnish the seed and agree to pay a certain price per ton for ears of corn in the green state. In this neighborhood they have been paying eight dollars per ton for ears with the husks on. Many farmers think it does not pay to grow it for less than ten dollars per ton. Of course much depends on the yield per acre. On ordinary farm land with ordinary culture, the yield is small, and the expense of gathering the crop absorbs nearly all the profits; but with a good crop, the profit at ten dollars per ton is entirely satisfactory, especially if you take the value of the stalks into consideration. It is a good crop to commence with in the field-garden; it brings in a little ready money every few days at a season when we are quite apt to need it.

POP-CORN.

Pop-corn is a small variety grown exclusively for popping. It is rarely fed to animals; though I am not sure that if we could invent some cheap and expeditious method of popping it on a large scale, it would not pay well in many cases to grow this corn and pop it for young animals or those which are sick. A little pig takes very kindly to pop-corn, after it is popped, and I have no doubt it is good for him, and if any of the boys wish to show their pigs at the fair, after they have given the pig a good square meal, and after he has eaten all he will, his pigship would enjoy a dessert of pop-corn, either plain or sweetened with molasses.

The cultivation of pop-corn is as easy and simple as that of ordinary field corn, but when they first come up, the plants are smaller and weaker, and for this reason it is desirable to plant pop-corn on a dry, warm, sandy soil. The kernels are very small, and I have found that in planting, one is apt to drop too many seeds in the hill. Pop-corn may be planted in hills three feet apart each way, and the land cultivated both ways with a horse-hoe, or it may be planted in rows three feet apart, and the seed drilled in, afterwards thinning out the plants to six or eight inches apart in the row. Pop-corn needs good soil and clean cultivation. I cut my crop with a reaper and tie it into bundles like wheat; set the bundles in a stook in the field until well cured, and if too busy to husk it in the fall, draw in the bundles and put them on an airy scaffold in the barn, and husk out the corn at my leisure.

CORN-SALAD.

Some might think that Corn-salad was a variety of corn grown for salad. In England wheat is called "corn," and corn-salad is supposed to derive its name from the fact that the plant grows among winter wheat. It is a very hardy plant and will, if sown in the fall, usually stand the winter and will start to grow in the spring, even earlier than spinach. It is a substitute, to some extent, for both lettuce and spinach. One of its popular names is "Lamb's Lettuce." It is a very easily raised plant, and is a favorite salad with those who like it. The cultivation is very simple. For spring use, sow early in September, in rows fifteen inches apart, dropping the seeds an inch apart in the row. Protect the plants in winter by lightly covering them with straw or litter. When used as a substitute for spinach, the land cannot be made too rich. For summer, sow in rows, fifteen inches apart, as early as the ground can be put into good condition; hoe, and thin out the plants to two or three inches apart; gather when young and tender,

Fig. 4.—CORN-SALAD.

and sow another bed a week or ten days later for succession. The seed is small, and should not be covered more than half an inch deep.

CRESS, OR PEPPER-GRASS.

Cress is very nice if grown rapidly, and is gathered before it runs to seed. It should have very rich land, be sown in rows wide enough apart to admit the use of a hoe, and about half an inch apart in the row. Sow as early as the ground can be worked in the spring, and each week afterwards for a succession.

WATER CRESS.

There are many places where Water Cress could be grown as a market crop with great profit. The real point is, to get low land which can be drained on the one hand, and flooded on the other. Ditches may be dug from the main stream, two or three feet wide, and deep enough to allow the water to flow in to the depth of two to six inches. In these ditches sow or plant the water cress. For your own use, cress can be obtained in ample abundance by sowing it in any shallow natural stream. A convenient plan is to scatter a little cress seed on the surface of the water, and let it float down stream. When the stream is once stocked nothing more is needed. It is a pity that water cress is not better known and more generally used, as it is one of the most healthful and delicious of salads.

CUCUMBERS.

Cucumbers, when grown in a hot-bed, will stand a good deal of heat, and their successful management requires some experience. It is usual to plant one hill of cucumbers to each sash, after using the hot-bed for starting other seeds in boxes, which can be removed when the cucumbers require more room. For out-door culture, early plants can be started in the hot-bed or in the house; six or eight seeds can be sown in some fine mould in a three-inch pot, and when the weather has become settled, the plants can be carefully turned out of the pot with all the soil adhering to the roots, and transferred to a well-prepared hill in the garden. For a few days, the plants should be covered with a frame or bottomless box having a piece of cotton cloth tacked over the top. Before the plants are turned out, the pots should be placed in a vessel containing some blood-warm water, two or three inches deep, and allowed to remain until the ball of earth is thoroughly saturated; this is far better than watering after they are transplanted.

Cucumbers delight in a warm, rich, mellow soil. For

field culture, a good plan is to mark off the ground into rows, four feet apart each way, then run a double mould-board plow along the mark, both ways. Put one or two good forkfuls of well-rotted manure where these furrows cross each other; then with a hoe, or potato hook, break up the manure very fine, and work it into the soil. Turn the soil back again on top of the manure with a plow, going on both sides of the row lengthwise and crosswise; follow the plow with a roller, going both ways of the rows. By doing this, the hills will be four feet apart each way, with manure underneath, and a bed of rich, mellow soil for the seed. I find it desirable, after using the roller, to go over the piece again with a four-foot marker, both ways, as this insures straight rows. Drop ten or twelve seeds in each hill, and after the plants are well up, and have got pretty well out of the reach of the Striped-bug, gradually thin them out, until in the end, you leave only four of the strongest plants in each hill. The after cultivation consists simply in working the soil with a cultivator or one-horse plow, both ways between the rows, removing all weeds from the hills with a hoe, at the same time pulling up a little fresh soil around the plants if necessary.

Another plan is, to mark off the land into rows four or five feet apart, run the double mould-board plow along the mark, spread the manure in the furrow, and cover it up by running the plow on both sides of the row; then roll, mark the land again, and drill in the seed in the mark just over the manure. Some may think it unnecessary to go over the land the second time with the marker, but it is very important to have the rows straight, as any boy will find when he undertakes to run a cultivator within an inch of the plants in the row. In drilling in the seed, set the drill to drop a seed each two or three inches, and to cover not over an inch deep. As the plants grow, keep them well cultivated, and thin out until you

CUCUMBERS.

have them from eight to ten inches apart in the row. There will often be two or three plants close together in the row, and if there are no others for fifteen or eighteen inches on each side, I should let them all grow.

Another plan, and I think on the whole the best, is to prepare the land just as thoroughly as you are able; spread a quantity of manure on the surface, say fifteen or twenty loads per acre; spread it evenly, and then go over it two or three times with a smoothing harrow, and if it pulls any of the manure into heaps, re-spread them and continue harrowing and rolling until the whole surface soil is as fine and mellow as a garden. In fact it is a garden—at any rate we wish to introduce garden culture on the farm. Mark out the land into rows four or five feet apart, and then, with a two-horse plow, throw up two furrows on each side of the mark, and so continue until the work is all done. In this way you will get a bed of light, mellow, well-manured soil in rows of four or five feet apart; roll the land, mark it once more, and drill in the seed.

Fig. 5. WHITE SPINE.

Fig. 6.—EARLY GREEN CLUSTER.

Cucumbers are sometimes grown on sod land. The land is marked out in rows, four or five feet apart both ways, and the seed planted in hills made with a hoe. If the land is in good condition, or if two tablespoonsfuls of superphosphate are scattered in each hill, you will be likely to have a good crop, with very few weeds to trouble you.

The leading varieties are Early Russian, Early Green Cluster, Early Frame, Early White Spine and Improved Long Green. The latter two varieties are extensively grown for the pickle factories, as well as for market and home use. The pickle factories, as a rule, however, prefer the White Spine. In this neighborhood, they pay from one dollar to one dollar and a half per thousand for the cucumbers, according to the size; a barrel of small ones contains about five thousand, for which they pay five dollars. Of the larger size, a barrel holds from one thousand two hundred to one thousand six hundred, for which they pay from one dollar and eighty cents to two dollars and forty cents per barrel. Some of my neighbors grow cucumbers for pickles on low, mucky soil, which is usually too wet to plow before the middle of June. They sometimes have good crops when they plant as late as the middle of July. It would, of course, be better to drain the land and plant earlier.

EGG PLANT.

Egg Plant, in this section, needs to be started in the hot-bed or in a box in the house, and, as the plants re-

Fig. 7.—NEW YORK IMPROVED PURPLE EGG PLANT.

quire a warm soil when set out in the garden, the seeds should not be sown in the house or hot-bed until the first or second week in April. Select a warm, sunny spot in the garden, and make the soil very loose and mellow, and moderately rich. Set the plants about thirty inches apart, keep the ground clean, and as they grow, draw a little fresh soil to them. Keep a sharp lookout for the Colorado-beetle or Potato-bug, as this likes the Egg-plant quite as well as it does potatoes, and if not destroyed will ruin the crop. The best variety is the New York Improved Purple.

ENDIVE.

Endive is a very hardy plant, easily grown, and when properly blanched makes an excellent salad. It can be sown at any time from March to August, but as it is usually eaten late in the fall, it is commonly sown in June or July, in rows twelve to fifteen inches apart, and the plants thinned out to a foot distant in the row. The blanching can be done in any way which excludes the light. The usual method is by gathering the leaves together and tying them at the top.

KOHL RABI.

Kohl Rabi is a variety of the cabbage, but it looks more like a turnip. It has been called the Turnip-rooted Cabbage. It is grown as a substitute for cabbage. It will stand dry weather better than turnips, yields equally well, and is quite as nutritious. It can be transplanted easily, but it is usually sown, like the turnip, where it is to remain. It can be profitably grown as a field crop for stock. Unlike the turnip it does not impart an unpleasant flavor to the milk when fed to cows. The preparation of the land, cultivation and harvesting, are similar to that required

Fig. 8.—KOHL RABI.

for ruta baga or Swedes. If any thing, the land should be richer and the seeds sown a little earlier. The best variety for stock or for table use, is the Large White or Large Green. For table use these should be grown quickly and used before they become stringy, which they will be apt to be if allowed to get larger than a teacup.

LETTUCE.

Every body raises Lettuce. While no plant is more easily grown, comparatively few people have it in perfection. The reason for this is three-fold. The soil is

Fig. 9.
"THE DEACON" LETTUCE.

Fig. 10.
COS LETTUCE.

not made rich enough, it is not thoroughly cultivated and hoed, and the plants are left entirely too close together. As an out-door crop, lettuce can be sown in the spring as early as the weather will permit. I have sown it in February, and though we had very severe weather afterwards, the plants were not injured by the frost. In the same field, however, the same variety, "The Deacon," sown April 14th, was just as large by the first of June as that sown in February. The best way with this, as with other hardy crops, is to sow as early as the ground can be brought into good condition, but not earlier.

My own plan in raising lettuce is, to make the land as fine and mellow as possible, and drill in the seed in rows, twenty-one inches apart. This is wide enough to admit the use of the horse-hoe. As soon as the rows can be traced, we go throngh with the cultivator, and in the course of a few days go through again; the object being to make the soil as loose and mellow as possible. I have gone through the rows three or four times with a cultivator before the plants were large enough to be thinned out with a hoe. This thinning out is the point necessary for success. It seems a great waste of seeds, of plants, and of land, to thin out the plants to eight or ten inches apart, but it is the true plan. You must dash your hoe through them boldly, cutting out the plants so that they will stand the width of the hoe apart; then with the hoe push out all the surplus ones. An ordinary hoe slants too much forward to do the work properly; you should heat the shank of the hoe, and bend it until the blade is nearly at right angles with the handle. For thinning out turnips, beets, mangels, etc., such a hoe will enable you to do the work without often resorting to thinning out the plants with the fingers. If the land is in proper condition, and you have a good variety, you will get a splendid crop of the largest and finest heads of lettuce, from the last of June to the middle of September.

MELONS—MUSK.

A few hills of Musk Melons can be started in the hot-bed or in the house, as recommended for cucumbers, and when the ground is warm, the plants can be set out in the open ground and shaded for a few days, until they get finally started. On a farm where land is abundant, the better plan is, to put in the melon seed in the open ground as soon as the soil is in good working condition. You may lose half your seed and be obliged to replant, but in three years out of four, you will get as good and as early a crop as you would by transplanting from the hot-bed. The mistake people make is, in not using seed enough. You ought to sow at least three times as many as you think you will need, even of the best of seed. Melons are not all of the best quality, and if you have more than you need, you can reject those which do not please you. We do not expect every apple on a tree to be perfect, and we need not expect every melon on the vine to be of the choicest quality. The methods recommended for the cultivation of cucumbers are generally adapted to the production of melons. If possible, the land should be made even richer for melons than for cucumbers. I have never yet seen land too rich for them. Plant largely and sow thickly, so that if the seed all grows, you can thin out the weak plants as directed for cucumbers. The best varieties are: the Early Christiana, the Nutmeg, Green Citron, White Japanese, and Casaba. Of the first three, Nutmeg, Christiana, and Citron, the best variety, in my judgment, is the one of

Fig. 11.—VARIETIES OF MUSKMELONS.
PROLIFIC NUTMEG.
CASABA.
WHITE JAPANESE.
NUTMEG.

which you happen to plant the most largely. If you have a large crop you can select delicious melons from either of these varieties.

MELONS—WATER.

Watermelons can be grown as easily as pumpkins or corn, but you can not grow corn and watermelons together. The land must be entirely devoted to the melons, and the mistake that people make, is, they try to grow melons and thistles on the same ground. The thistles pump up a large quantity of water from the soil, and when we have dry, hot weather, the melons are left without sufficient moisture. The weather can not be too hot for this crop, provided it has sufficient moisture and plant food. People are apt to think that if they keep the soil clean immediately around the hills, the rest of the land can be suffered to produce weeds. This is a great mistake; the roots of the melons are at least as long as the vines, and in our dry, hot climate, they need all the moisture the land contains. The distance apart at which it is best to plant watermelons depends on the climate. In this section, they will do well planted in hills or rows four or five feet apart, but as we go south, we must increase the distance. One of my correspondents in Texas, wrote me that his watermelons completely covered the ground, even when they are planted fifteen or twenty feet apart.

I have grown excellent watermelons on light, rich, sandy soil, in rows five feet apart. We drilled in the seed with an ordinary garden drill, using the hole made for sowing corn. As the plants grow, thin out, leaving them from eight to fifteen inches apart in the row, just as you happen to find them. If the plants are thin, and you find two or three near together, leave them all to grow if necessary. If the land is rich enough, and you keep it thoroughly cultivated and free from weeds, you may expect a great crop of melons, and if you don't get it, try again. When the vines commence to run, the weeds also begin to grow, and you may think that you can not get through the rows with a cultivator; but by going ahead of the horse, you may move the vines out of the way, and leave plenty of room for the horse and cultivator. Make thorough work, going twice in the row, or as often as is necessary to kill every weed, and break up the hard, dry soil. Work it until it is as mellow as a garden, and if there are any weeds left which you can not reach with a cultivator, cut them out with a hoe, or pull them by hand.

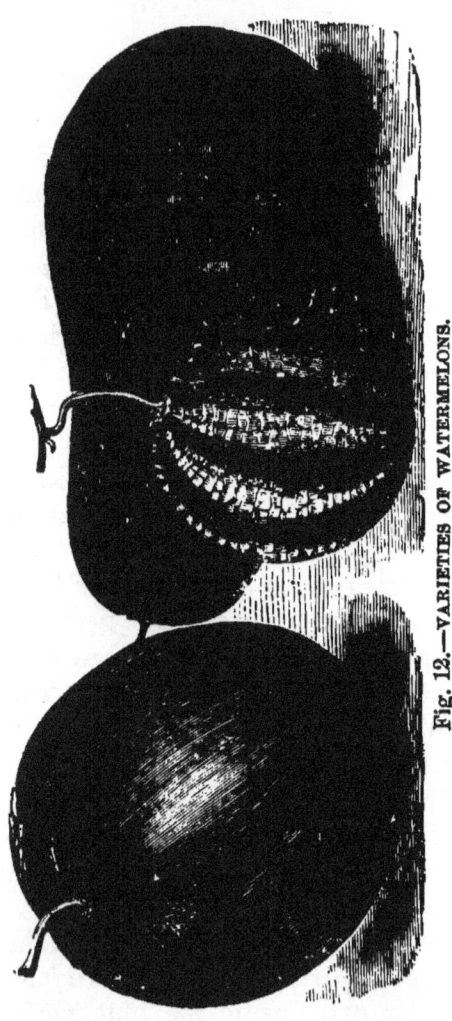

Fig. 12.—VARIETIES OF WATERMELONS. MOUNTAIN SWEET. CITRON. BLACK SPANISH.

Watermelons may be planted in hills, and the land prepared as recommended for cucumbers, except that it is necessary to make the hills wider apart. The method, however, of plowing the land into ridges, or hills, both ways, is just as applicable to watermelons and muskmelons as to cucumbers. The best varieties are: the Black Spanish, Ice Cream, and Mountain Sweet. They can be planted a little earlier than muskmelons, but there is nothing gained by doing it before the land can be put into the finest condition. A common mistake in planting melons and cucumbers is, to cover the seed too deep; half an inch is quite deep enough for both muskmelons and cucumbers. Watermelons, the seed of which is much larger, can be deeper, but much depends on the nature and condition of the soil. Many a hill of melon seed is literally smothered by being covered with an inch of damp soil which bakes on the surface, while two inches of dry, mellow sandy soil would do no harm.

CITRON WATERMELON.

This variety is grown exclusively for preserving. The fruit is round, skin light, and dark-green, handsomely striped and marbled; a few hills should be planted in every garden. The cultivation is precisely the same as for other melons. It is the smaller of the melons on page 76.

MUSTARD.

For salad the cultivation of Mustard is the same as for cress. Sow in rows wide enough apart to admit the use of the hoe, dropping two or three seeds to each inch of row. For an early crop, select a warm, sandy soil, sow as early as the soil is dry and mellow, cover not more than one-quarter inch deep. In a week or ten days, sow another bed, and continue to do so at intervals for a succession. The

Fig. 13.—MUSTARD.

best variety for salad is the White Mustard. As a field crop this deserves attention; our climate is well adapted to its cultivation. As a crop for plowing under to enrich sandy soil, or to lighten and mellow a heavy one, White Mustard could often be used with special advantage. It can also be profitably grown for feeding to sheep on the land, or for feeding green to cows, pigs, and horses. A great crop can be grown for this purpose on good, mellow land; but unless the land is mellow, it is of no use to try it in our dry, hot climate. It may be sown as late as the first of July, and still give a large crop in September and October. It must be eaten before frost. After a severe frost, it is only fit for plowing under for a manure.

The better way is to sow about twenty pounds of seed per acre, in rows twenty-one inches apart, or far enough to admit the use of a horse-hoe. As soon as the plants appear, run the cultivator between the rows, and continue to cultivate at intervals, until the plants are fairly started. They grow slowly at first, but if the land is in good condition, when they are once started, they grow with great rapidity and will smother the weeds and leave the land remarkably clean.

NASTURTIUM.—TROPÆOLUM.

In our dry, hot climate, the Nasturtium or Indian Cress, can be grown with great ease and certainty. As the plants are very tender, the slightest frost injuring them, they should have a warm, dry soil, moderately rich, and kept free from weeds. There are two varieties usually grown, one of which is a climber, and will run up on a pole or trellis for eight or ten feet. The other is a dwarf variety, growing from one to two feet high. The latter may be allowed to trail on the ground, or be furnished with a few short sticks. The nasturtium is grown for both ornament and use. The flowers are very beautiful, and the seed-pods are pickled and used as a substitute for capers. A row of the dwarf kind, with a few short sticks eighteen inches long, and stuck a foot apart, not on the sides, but in the center of the row, is a charming addition to any garden.

It is desirable to get the plants as early as possible, but they are very tender, and if we sow early, we run the risk of having them destroyed by frost; but we can well afford to take the risk. Sow two rows. The seed is cheap. Sow one row at the same time you plant corn. The seed is large and may be covered from one to two inches deep, according to the nature of the soil. The earlier you plant, and the heavier the soil the shallower should be the seed. A good plan is, to make a double row, just as we sometimes do for peas. The rows may be about four inches apart, with one seed to each two inches of row. The sticks can be placed between these narrow rows. If more than one of these double rows is needed, the large climbing nasturtium should be planted in rows five feet apart, but the dwarf may be planted in rows thirty inches apart. The second planting, which should never be neglected, may be made about the time we plant beans.

OKRA—OR GUMBO.

At the North it is desirable to raise Okra plants in a hot-bed, or in a box in the house, and transplant them to the garden about the middle of May. If the seed is sown out of doors, select a loose, warm soil, with a southern exposure. There are two varieties, the Dwarf and Tall; the former is the best. Plant the dwarf kind in rows thirty inches apart, and from eight to ten inches in the row, or sufficiently wide to admit the free use of the hoe. The tall kind should be in rows three feet apart, and the plants a foot in the row. After they are well started, nothing is required except to keep the land free from weeds. The principal use of okra is in soups. The green pods are used for this purpose; they contain much mucilage which thickens the soup, and imparts an agreeable flavor. It is regarded as heathful and nutritious. The ripe seeds roasted and ground have sometimes been used as a substitute for coffee.

ONIONS.

Great improvements have been made in the cultivation of Onions, and still greater improvements are yet to be made, especially in our methods of drilling in the seed and hoeing, and weeding the crop. I have for several years sown my onion seed in rows, from twenty-one to twenty-five inches apart, and cultivated with a horse-hoe. It is a great saving of labor, but many will object to the plan, because they think they can get a much heavier yield per acre when the seed is sown in closer rows, say a foot apart. Such is probably the case. It is a question of land *versus* labor. The improvement I want to see made is, in having a drill which will sow four rows at a time. It would be better, probably, to have the two center rows twenty inches apart, and the other rows a foot apart. This would give plenty of room for a quiet horse to walk between the center rows. We should have the piece sown as follows: there would be one space twenty inches wide, and then four rows a foot apart, each, and then another wide space of twenty inches, and so on. We must then have a cultivator or horse-hoe that would go between these rows. It must be the exact size of the drill, and provided with a steerage attachment which would give us control of the hoes or cultivator teeth. If the drill was rigid, if there was any deviation from a straight line in any of the drills, there would be the same deviation in all of them, and if we could avoid cutting up the plants in one row, we should also avoid doing so in the other three rows. Such a drill and cultivator combined would be not only very useful for sowing and cultivating onions, but for many other farm and garden crops, such as turnips, beets, parsnips, carrots, etc.

Until we have such a machine, we must do the best we can with the tools we now have. In fact, a farmer who undertakes to raise onions for the first time as a field crop, could hardly use such a machine as I have proposed, he would require to have his land much cleaner and smoother, and freer from stones than would likely to be the case on any ordinary farm. Land for onions has to be made to order. Onions do better on old onion land than when they are raised on any ordinary soil for the first time. Nearly all other crops do better in rotation, than when grown year after year on the same land. It is not clear why onions should be an exception. I think chemistry and plant food have far less to do with it than the mechanical state of the land. If a man or a boy would bestow the necessary amount of labor in preparing and enriching the land, I see no reason to doubt that he could get just as good a crop the first year, as he could the second, third, or tenth year; but no man will do it; perhaps a boy may. There was some excuse for men in years gone by—they had not the necessary tools. With our modern implements we can place land in wonderfully fine condition, at comparatively little expense, the first year; but much of the work ought to be done in the autumn. Suppose you try how rich, and mellow, you can make an acre of land this fall. It does not make very much difference how you do it. The first thing, however, is to get off all the stones, and stumps, and rubbish. If a harrow will do it any good, harrow it; if not, plow it, and then roll, and harrow, and roll again, until every lump is broken that the harrow and roller can reach; then plow again, and if you should turn under twenty or thirty loads of well-rotted manure, so much the better. A hundred loads to the acre will do no harm, provided it is thoroughly mixed with the soil. In fact, it is probably this intimate admixture of the manure with the soil, that makes old onion land so much better than new. Work in, therefore, all the manure you can; you can not put on too much, and you can not, at all events you certainly will not, work it in too thoroughly.

If the land is properly prepared in the autumn, it is not necessary or desirable to plow it again in the spring; it might be gone over with a gang-plow or cultivator, or if the soil is light, a good harrow will be sufficient. It is very essential to get in the seed as soon as the frost is out of the ground. In fact, the onions may be sown to advantage as soon as the first two or three inches are thawed out and moderately dry, even though the sub-soil is still a mass of frozen earth. Onions are quite hardy, and will stand an ordinary frost without injury.

In sowing onions with a drill, it is very desirable to have the tube, or coulter, which makes the drill row in which the seed is deposited, as narrow as possible. It was thought at one time better to scatter the seed in a wide drill mark, but there is nothing to be gained by it, and the wider it is, the greater space is there which we can not reach with the hoe, and which we must weed with the fingers. Our drill makers do not seem to understand this, or instead of the rough cast-iron shank, which many of them have hitherto furnished, they would make a bright, sharp, narrow steel coulter, which would not clog or make too wide a drill mark.

As soon as the rows can be traced, go through with a hoe. It will do the onions good, even if there are no weeds. Some people recommend going over the land with a steel rake, but I have never yet had sufficient courage to rake my crop of onions hard enough to kill the weeds. If you do the work yourself, I think it is very likely that there are times when a steel rake would destroy millions of weeds without injuring the onions. On the whole, however, I think we had better depend on a sharp, bright hoe, skillfully used on each side of the rows, pulling out with the fingers any weeds that may be left in the row. If you have a large crop, and there is danger that the weeds may get the start of you, it is better not to stop to pull out the weeds at the first hoeing; go through the patch with a hoe, and then, when the whole piece is once hoed, go over it again, hoeing and hand-weeding at the same time. It is generally necessary to weed onions twice. The only safe rule is, to hoe and weed as often as is necessary to kill every weed, and even if there are no weeds visible, it pays to run a cultivator or hoe between the rows once a week until the onions are five or six inches high. Success in raising onions depends largely on three things: rich land, early sowing, and clean cultivation.

The best varieties are the Yellow Danvers, Early Red Globe, White Globe, and the Large Red Wethersfield. The Early Red Globe can be grown successfully where the later varieties, like the Large Wethersfield, are apt to run up to scallions. Scallions are the dread of the onion grower. A scallion is an onion with a thick neck. Instead of forming a bulb early in the season, the top then withering down, the onion keeps on growing, throwing out a great mass of roots, forming a long, thick neck, with a comparatively immature bulb. Sometimes scallions are the result of poor seed. I do not mean seed that will not grow, but that which is raised from late, immature onions, not good enough to send to market. But no respectable seed-grower ever raises such seed, and we must look for other causes to learn why onions so frequently turn to scallions. Late sowing is the most frequent cause;

neglecting to hoe and weed the crop when young, is another cause, and possibly, poor land has something to do with it. It is usual to sow five pounds of onion seed per acre. But I am aware that this does not tell you how thick you must sow the seed. I should set the drill to drop about three seeds to each inch of row. It is far better to have an onion crop too thick than too thin. In hoeing and weeding, no matter how careful you may be, more or less onions will be destroyed.

The market demand is not so much for large onions as formerly. It is far better to have three moderate-sized bulbs than one very large one, and the old practice of thinning onions so as to leave only one bulb to each three or four inches of row, is now abandoned by all experienced growers. Onions will grow in bunches, three, four, or five in a bunch, and if the land is rich enough, and the rows are sufficiently wide apart, a dozen, fifteen, or even twenty onions can be grown on each foot of row.

The Onion-maggot is sometimes quite troublesome. It rarely troubles me, but one of my neighbors, who raises large crops of onions on what was formerly a Black-Ash swamp, and which is even still only partially drained, occasionally suffers much loss. He thinks an application of four hundred pounds of salt per acre, sown broadcast early in the spring, will kill the maggot; perhaps so, perhaps not. The salt, however, will do no harm, and may otherwise do good, even if it does not always kill the maggot. I have known Peruvian guano to be used for the same purpose with decided advantage; and so with superphosphate of lime, or any other good fertilizer. Any thing which will promote rapid growth, will lessen the chances of injury from maggots or loss from scallions.

Perhaps a word should be said in regard to the best land for onions. In point of fact there is no best land for them; you must make the land. Onions will grow on all kinds of soil, ranging from the most spongy muck to the heaviest clay. Probably the most profitable onion ground would be a mucky swamp, with a never failing stream running through it, with sufficient fall to afford good drainage three feet deep. If such a swamp were thoroughly subdued, drain-tiles laid two and a half to three feet deep, every three or four rods, and then a dam built across this stream, with a gate which could be elevated or lowered at pleasure, the most magnificent crops of onions could be grown every year, with comparatively little labor. In the spring, the gate of course would be lifted, and the under-drains, even though they had to discharge into the swollen stream, would remove the stagnant water, and leave the surface dry and firm, and the onions could be sown as soon as we had a few fine days in spring. When dry weather set in, and the crop needed more moisture, shut down the gate, and as the water rose in the stream it would flow back into the under drains, and the dry, porous, mucky soil would suck it up like a sponge, and the dryer and hotter the weather the more rapidly would the onions grow. We might safely calculate on getting from such a soil an average crop, year after year, of one thousand bushels per acre. Onions will sell readily in the autumn, shipped direct from the field, for seventy-five cents to one dollar per bushel, and you can tell as well as I, whether it would pay to make the improvement suggested. Onion land is often rented on shares, the owner furnishing half the seed, and half the manure, and the tenant doing all the work, and giving the landowner half the crop. On such a piece of land as I have described, the net profit to the owner would average at least three hundred and sixty dollars an acre, which is six per cent. interest on six thousand dollars.

ONION SETS.

Onion Sets, so called, are simply small onions. If a small onion is set out in the fall or in the spring, it will grow and produce either one very large onion, or two or three good sized ones. In the Southern States, and in many sections of the South-west, it is not easy to grow onions direct from the seed, or "black seed" as the growers often call it, to distinguish it from the sets. There onions are grown from sets, and there is a large demand for these small onions or sets, the price ranging from five dollars to ten dollars per bushel. The smaller the onions, provided the bulbs are mature and well formed, the more valuable they are, because a given number will not only plant more land, but there is less likelihood of their running up to seed. Onion sets are grown in the same way as ordinary onions, except that they are sown very much thicker.

Many people have an idea that the way to raise onion sets is to sow the seed late in the spring, and to select rather poor, sandy land. This is a mistake; they need good, warm, dry and rich soil, and the earlier the seeds are sown the better. In this section, the crop should be ripe not later than the first of August. It is a good plan to prepare the ground in the fall, as recommended for onions; then in the spring, mark off the land into rows, thirty inches apart, taking pains to make the rows straight, then drill in six rows of seed from an inch and a half to two inches apart alongside of the mark; set the drill to drop five or six seeds in each inch of row, in each of the six rows. In other words, when the set of rows is sown, you should have from thirty to thirty-six seeds in each lineal inch. The advantage of the plan is, that you can use the horse-hoe or cultivator between the wide rows, and between the narrow rows a sharp pointed onion-hoe can be used to break the crust, and kill the weeds; weeds which can not be reached with the hoe should be pulled out by hand. It is absolutely essential to keep the crop clean. The object is, to stimulate growth on the one hand, and to produce early maturity on the other, with a tendency to produce bulbs. We wish to raise dwarf onions. We can not do this unless every condition for the growth of the plant, except root pruning and excessive crowding, is favorable. It is not easy to keep onion sets during the winter, and in fact the better way is to plant the sets in the fall. They will stand the winter without injury, and give a larger crop. If, however, you wish to keep the sets through the winter, do not put them in a damp cellar, but in a dry loft, which can be kept as near the freezing point as possible, so as to prevent them from starting to grow. Freezing will not injure them, provided you can keep them from thawing until they are wanted in the spring.

RAISING ONION SEED.

It is a very important matter to have good seed, and I recommend my young friends to select a few of their choicest and best onions and set them out every fall for seed. Onions for seed can be set in spring or autumn, but the latter is the best time. And here I would like to tell the boys an important discovery which I think I have made, and which I am almost tempted to keep for my own use and profit, as I think there is money in it. I have for the last eighteen years been growing seed of the Yellow Danvers variety. I selected the very best bulbs from a large crop each year, and I succeeded in getting a strain of the choicest seed. It produced the finest onions, but I could get scarcely any seed. When I raised the seed it was very valuable; but there was so little of it, that it has sometimes cost me one hundred dollars per pound. The onions were so good that they would not produce seed. The discovery that I think I have made is this: sow the seed in the spring in the usual way, except that you sow it very thickly; the object being to get small bulbs. Set these small onions out in the fall, and let them produce large onions, rejecting any that go to seed at that time. The next fall, set out these large onions for seed. The way we do this, is to make the land very rich, thoroughly mixing the manure with the soil and have it as clean and mellow as possible. Mark off the land with a common corn-marker in rows forty-two inches apart; set out the onions in these rows, four or five inches apart, or so near that they will almost touch each other in the row, press them down into the mellow soil, and cover carefully with the hoe or plow. If the plow is used, follow with a hoe so as to be sure that every bulb is well covered to the depth of two or three inches. The best time here to set out onions for seed is about the first of October. Nothing more needs to be done until spring, when the soil must be thoroughly and repeatedly cultivated, and not a weed suffered to grow. The seed is gathered by cutting off the heads into baskets, and spreading them out on canvas to dry. Thrash with a flail, and clean by running through a fanning mill.

THE POTATO ONION.

The cultivation of Potato Onions is similar to that of onion sets. The small potato onions are planted early in spring, in rows fifteen inches apart, and four to five inches distant in the row; keep the land clean, and that is all there is to be done. Each small bulb will make a large one. The next spring set out some of the large bulbs that have been saved for the purpose, and each will give a cluster of small ones to be planted the following year. This is the usual routine, but generally a share of those planted will split up into several small ones instead of making one large onion.

THE TOP, OR TREE ONION.

When an ordinary onion is set out in autumn or in spring, it throws up a stalk with a large head of flowers, followed by seed. A Top-onion grows in precisely the same manner, but it throws up a stalk, on the top of which, instead of seed, we have a bunch or cluster of small onions. When these small bulbs are set out in the fall or spring, they give us a crop of very early green onions. The objection to the top onion is, that when ripe it does not keep well, and should be used in the fall.

PARSLEY.

Parsley seed is very slow in germinating, and it is desirable to sow it as early in the spring as possible. The soil should be prepared in the fall, and the seed sown as soon as the frost is out of the ground. Sow in rows fifteen inches apart, dropping three or four seeds to each inch of row; keep the ground hoed and entirely free from weeds. Thin out the plants to two inches apart in the row. There is a rapidly increasing demand for parsley, not only for garnishing, but for flavoring soups, etc. The best variety for the garden is the Extra Double-Curled. In Europe, parsley is often sown with a mixture of grasses and clover, as a pasture for sheep; for this purpose, the common straight-leaved variety is the best. The seed is cheaper and the yield larger. Sheep are very fond of parsley, and it is supposed to give an agreeable flavor to the mutton. Parsley is biennial; if sown this spring it makes only leaves, but the next year it runs up to seed. During the winter and spring, previous to its going to seed, a small bed would afford an abundance. But if you have no parsley at all in the garden, and wish a supply early in the summer, a good plan is, to sow the seed in a box in the house, in February, and transplant it to the

Fig. 14.—PARSLEY.

open ground as soon as the weather is suitable. It is a hardy, vigorous plant, and grows rapidly when fairly started, but is slow until the plants get firm hold of the soil.

PARSNIP.

Taking one year with another, there are few crops which the farm-gardener can raise to greater advantage and profit, in proportion to the labor required, than the Parsnip. It is hardier than the carrot, can be sown earlier, requires less weeding, yields quite as many or more bushels to the acre, and the roots, if we wish, can be left in the soil all winter without injury. If desired, parsnips can be sown in the fall; the only precaution necessary being to put in about twice as much seed as you would in the spring, so that if any of the plants are killed by the winter, there will be enough left. The usual time of sowing parsnips, and probably the best time, is about that for planting Indian corn. There is nothing to be gained by sowing before the land can be brought into the very best possible condition. On my own farm, we usually sow about the first of June, in rows twenty-one inches apart, sowing about three seeds to each inch of drill. It pays to sow thickly, as the plants come up better and hold the weeds in check, and they can then be thinned out with a sharp-pointed hoe to three inches apart in the row, at the same time cutting out many of the weeds. Keep the ground thoroughly cultivated and hoed, and if the land is rich and well prepared, you can hardly fail of getting a large crop. As before stated, parsnips can be left in the ground all winter, and those not required before spring are better if left out. Those needed for use in winter and early spring, must be dug in the fall and kept in the cellar, mixed with sand, or what is better still, pitted in the field, or on some sandy knoll near the house.

It quite often happens that parsnips will bring a very high price in early spring, before the frost is out of the ground, and those who have them in pits can sell at a large profit. Last spring, I was offered seventy-five cents a bushel for my entire crop. It is not at all a difficult matter to raise from six hundred to eight hundred bushels to the acre. True, there are required good soil, deeply and thoroughly worked, plenty of manure, early sowing, good seed, and good cultivation. The best variety for deep, rich soils, is the Long White Dutch, and for a somewhat shallower soil, the Hollow Crown. It is very important to get good fresh seed, as that which is more than one year old will nearly always fail to grow.

TO RAISE PARSNIP SEED.

Where the crop of Parsnip seed is not injured by the caterpillar (*Depressaria cicutella*), its production is easy and profitable. But it is desirable to take more pains in raising it than is sometimes given to the crop. The seed should never be grown from plants which have been left in the ground all winter, and suffered to throw up their stalks where they stand, as it is impossible to tell which are and which are not the best formed roots. The roots should be taken up in autumn, and carefully selected, rejecting all that show any disposition to fork or throw out fangs. The smoothest, handsomest, and best formed roots only, should be selected for seed. Prepare the land the previous autumn, plowing it not less than ten inches deep, and working in a good coat of well-rotted manure, not less than twenty tons per acre. The more thoroughly the land can be worked the better; then, as early in the spring as the soil and season will admit, mark out the land in rows, forty-two inches apart, and with a good plow throw out a deep, straight furrow. Set out the parsnips six to eight inches apart in the furrow, and, if necessary, use a crowbar to make holes for them; then turn the furrow back again upon the parsnips, finishing the work with a hoe, taking care to pull the soil well up to the crowns. If the soil is loose and mellow, it may be half an inch or so deep on top of the roots. Nothing more is required, except to keep the land well cultivated and hoed, as long as you can get between the rows with a horse. If any weeds are left, they must be pulled out by hand, or cut off with the hoe. If the caterpillars appear, there is nothing to be done but to give them a gentle pressure with the finger and thumb. If they bury themselves in the umbels, do not wait to ascertain whether the caterpillar is in the nest or not, give it the benefit of the doubt. I have pinched many a nest with a good deal of satisfaction, and with much profit to the crop of seed.

PEAS.

The market gardener, and in fact all the gardeners, take great pains to get Peas as early as possible. Fortunately the seed is very hardy and will germinate at a low temperature, except some of the late and large varieties, such as the Veitch's Perfection. In three seasons out of four, the seed of these is apt to rot in the ground, but the moderately sized, early varieties, which, unfortunately are not, and I fear never can be, so sweet as the large and later kinds, can be planted the moment the frost is out of the ground. Last year I planted my peas in February, and I do not think one in a hundred failed to germinate. For early peas, therefore, it is necessary to prepare the soil the autumn previous, taking just as much pains as if you were going to sow the crop at that time. I would even mark out the rows where the seeds are to be sown; then in the spring, open a row, or drill, two or three inches wide with a hoe, about two inches deep, and sow the peas, not more than half an inch apart, or five or six peas to each lineal inch of this wide row. Thick seeding is very desirable, not only for early peas, but for nearly all early crops; the seeds in germinating give out heat, and when thick in the row or bed, they help to keep each other warm.

Early peas should be sown on the warmest and dryest land, it does not make much difference whether it is light or heavy, provided it is dry and can be readily worked in the spring without afterwards baking. A sandy loam, and from that to a light sand, is best, but whatever the character of the soil, a good crop of very early peas can not be grown unless it is rich. For a second early crop, it is not necessary to take so much pains; still, the better the soil and the better the preparation, with a liberal amount of manure, the more satisfactory will be the crop.

Fig. 15.—GREEN PEA PODS.

Sow as soon as the land can be got in good working condition; the earlier the better. Peas, as a rule, cannot be sown too early. The succession of crops should be looked after, by sowing varieties that are early, second early, medium and late, rather than by the time of sowing. In the garden we usually sow all except the dwarf varieties in rows, three to four feet apart, and stick brush on each side of the row for the peas to climb upon. This is done for the convenience of picking, and it may be that a larger yield is obtained.

In raising them on a large scale for picking green for market, or for the canning establishments, peas are never stuck or brushed. My own plan is to drill in the seed in a double row twenty-eight inches apart. We take a wheat drill which has coulters or tubes, seven inches apart; the two outside tubes we wire together, so that they are not more than two inches apart; the next three tubes are drawn up and shut off so that they will not sow; the next two tubes are wired together as before, and allowed to sow, and the next three tubes are shut off, and the next two outside tubes are wired together and allowed to sow. We thus sow three double rows at a time, and we have a space of fully two feet between the rows, in which we can use the cultivator or horse-hoe. The plan works admirably. I like to sow the peas thickly, and we set the drill so that, if all the tubes were running, we should sow four bushels per acre, but as there are twelve tubes in the drill, and we only sow with six, we use but two bushels per acre. This is thick enough, but it is not a bit too thick; I should prefer to sow thicker than this, rather than thinner. To succeed in raising green peas for market in this way, we must not expect a large crop on average farm land, with average farm treatment. We want the dryest and best of land. It should be free from stones and sticks, and in the very best mechanical condition, with a liberal supply of manure. The soil should be made ready the autumn previous, using only a gang-plow or cultivator in the spring. The roller and harrow should be used again and again, if necessary, until every clod is broken, and the surface soil is as loose and mellow as a garden. In fact, it is a garden, and we are proposing to grow a very important and profitable crop.

The best varieties for market are: the Extra Early Kent, for the earliest crop; Kentish Invicta, for the second early, and the Champion of England, or the White Marrowfat, for the last crop. In quality, Champion of England is by far the best variety. In the garden, for home use, we have many varieties of great merit. For the earliest crop, I know of nothing better than a good strain of Extra Early Kent. It has a dozen or more different names; the value of the alleged varieties depends on the care with which they are selected for seed. They have a constant tendency to degenerate on the one hand, or to improve on the other, and a skillful and experienced grower, by selecting the earliest peas and those which are the most wrinkled, can very soon obtain a strain of early peas which is certain to give satisfaction. If, on the other hand, all the earliest pods are picked off for your own table or for market, and those which are left used for seed, you will soon have a strain of Early Kent Peas that are no better than the Canada Creeper, or other small, round, smooth, common field pea. Peas do not mix, at any rate not readily or frequently, and a really new variety is rarely found. Some valuable new kinds have been obtained by artificial crossing.

Of late years, much attention has been paid to the introduction of dwarf varieties of peas, such as Tom Thumb, Little Gem, and the American Wonder. The advantages of the dwarf kinds are, that they do not need sticks, and two or three times as many rows can be sown on the land.

If, however, the only object of bushing is to lift up the peas to a convenient hight for picking, we gain nothing in this respect by sowing the dwarf kinds. It is quite as tiresome to pick pods from dwarf peas as it is from unbushed Early Kent, or Champion of England. Dwarf peas should not be sown in rows less than fifteen inches apart. The land should be rich, and kept well hoed and entirely free from weeds. Dwarf peas, if sown in close rows and the weeds allowed to grow, will not give satisfaction. Green peas, to be tender and sweet, must be grown rapidly, and for this they must have the richest of land, and the best of cultivation. It is quite an object to get a crop of peas late in the season, when the main crop is all gone. For this purpose, late varieties, such as Champion of England or Marrowfats are sown late in the spring. In three years out of four, however, these late sown, late varieties, are apt to mildew. The better way is to sow the early varieties in June or July. In the hands of a skillful and experienced gardener, peas are a very profitable crop. The price varies considerably, ranging from two dollars per bushel for the early, to fifty cents per bushel later in the season. The latter price is paid by the canning factories. It is a good plan to contract with a canning establishment to take all the peas after the price in market falls to seventy-five cents per bushel. Taking the whole crop together, the returns are quite satisfactory. It costs here fifteen cents per bushel to pick the peas.

BUGGY PEAS.

The principal insect enemy of the pea is the Weevil (*Bruchus pisi*). It is spreading very rapidly. Not long ago, peas grown in the northern latitudes and in Canada, were not injured by the Weevil. Now we get "buggy peas" from many places formerly free from this pest. There is nothing that we can do to check or destroy the Weevil after it is introduced. What we should all aim to do is, never to sow buggy peas. In time this would help us. Do not buy seed peas from any seedsman unless he will warrant them entirely free from bugs.

PEPPER—CAPSICUM.

Pepper, or Capsicum, is a tender plant. It does well in the Northern States after the plants are fairly started. Occasionally we can grow them by sowing the seed in the open ground, about the time we plant melons and cucumbers; but, as a rule, it is better to start the plants

Fig. 16.—PEPPER.—LARGE BELL OR BULL-NOSE.

in a hot-bed, or in a box in the house. When the ground is thoroughly warm, and all danger of frosty nights is passed, set them out carefully in the warmest, lightest, and best soil you have. Plant in rows twenty-four to thirty inches apart, and from twelve to fifteen inches apart in the rows. Keep the ground clean and mellow by the frequent use of the cultivator and hoe. The best variety is the Bell, or Bull-nosed. It is extensively used for pickling and for seasoning. Cayenne pepper, a smaller-fruited variety, is cultivated in the same way.

POTATOES.

As a garden crop, potatoes are seldom grown, except for the early market or for home use in summer. The later varieties are grown as a field crop. It often happens, however, that the gardener can plant potatoes on land from which some early crop has been removed. A very good crop can be grown here when planted as late as from June 15th to July 4th; but for late planting, it is best to use the early varieties. For an early crop, it will pay well to take considerable pains in preparing and manuring the soil. The land should be made ready the fall previous, and the moment the frost is out of the ground, plant the potatoes in rows twenty-four to thirty inches apart, and from ten to twelve inches apart in the row. If the land is very rich, and you intend to dig the potatoes as early as possible, thicker planting will give a larger crop, say rows eighteen inches apart, and the potatoes dropped eight inches apart in the row.

I have been in the habit, every year, of planting potatoes the first moment the land could be worked, and it has frequently happened that we had a very severe and long-continued frost afterwards, but the potatoes were never injured in the ground; they always came up strong and healthy. Occasionally we have a frosty night in the spring which cuts down our early potatoes, but those who plant moderately early are nearly as liable to be caught as those who plant just as early as possible.

Potatoes can be readily transplanted, and we frequently start a few hills in the hot-bed, and transplant them into the open ground when the tops are four or five inches high. By covering them with a hand-glass, or shading them for a few days with a muslin-covered box, these transplanted potatoes will give a very early crop. It need hardly be said that potatoes should be well cultivated and kept entirely free from weeds. For the early crops especially, the land must be very rich, and kept scrupulously clean and no bugs suffered to feed on the leaves.

The varieties are too numerous to mention, and every year brings new candidates for popular favor. The best early varieties that have been generally tried, are the Early Rose, and Early Vermont, which is so much like the Early Rose that it is difficult to tell them apart. The Beauty of Hebron is one of the newer varieties, early, productive; it is of good quality, and promises to be very desirable. Gardeners should stick to the well-tried sorts, testing the newer varieties only on a small scale.

PUMPKINS.

The common field pumpkin is usually grown as a secondary or stolen crop among corn. Careful farmers, however, who wish to cultivate their corn thoroughly, are getting out of the habit of planting pumpkins with the corn. They think it better to devote a piece of land entirely to the crop. A large yield can be produced in this way, and the pumpkins will be larger, sweeter, and better ripened. The better varieties of pumpkins can seldom be advantageously grown among corn. They should be planted alone, and the richer and the better the soil, and the more thoroughly it is worked previous to planting, the more profitable will be the crop. Plant in rows from eight to ten feet apart, and three to four feet apart in the rows, dropping eight or ten seeds in a hill. Afterward pull out all the weak plants, and those injured by the Striped-bug or Squash-bug, leaving three or four good strong plants in a hill. Keep the land clean by the frequent use of the cultivator and hoe as long as you can get between the rows of plants. The best variety for planting in the corn field is what is known as the Connecticut Field Pumpkin. For growing on land entirely devoted to the crop, the best varieties are the Connecticut Field, the Large Cheese, and the New Jersey Sweet Pumpkin. The Possum-nose Pumpkin is a new variety, which I obtained from the Hon. Horace Ankenny, of Ohio. It is best grown on land entirely devoted to it, though in Ohio and farther South it is grown among corn. It is very productive, a rampant grower, of good size, and is of good quality, but its greatest merit is, that it will keep the year round.

Fig. 17.—POSSUM-NOSE PUMPKIN.

RADISHES.

My own plan of raising radishes is, to prepare the land carefully in the fall, working in a good dressing of well-rotted manure. A light sandy loam is the best, but any soil that is dry, mellow and rich, will produce good radishes in a favorable season. New soil, full of leaf-mould, is particularly suitable for the crop.

Soil which has been well prepared in the fall we do not plow again in the spring. It is simply cultivated or gang-plowed, four or five inches deep, and repeatedly harrowed and rolled, until not a lump remains. We usually sow four hundred pounds of superphosphate of lime, broadcast, per

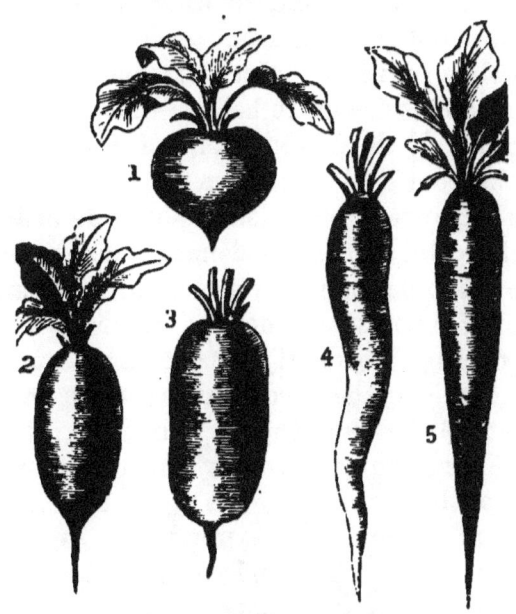

Fig. 18.—EARLY RADISHES.
1. Scarlet Turnip. 2. Rose Olive-Shaped. 3. French Breakfast. 4. Long White Naples. 5. Long Scarlet Short Top.

acre. Set a line for the first row, and sow the seed in shallow drills, twenty-one inches apart, dropping about three seeds to each inch of row. As the radishes come up quickly, no weeding, and very little hoeing will be required on clean, well-prepared land, but we run the horse-hoe repeatedly between the rows, commencing as soon as they can be traced, and repeat the operation twice a week. This thorough cultivation favors rapid growth, and with the aid of superphosphate and rich soil, soon enables the plant to get out of reach of the little Black-beetle.

It is very important to get good seed, raised from selected plants, for it is indeed exceedingly rare to buy seed that does not produce from ten to thirty per cent of poor, worthless radishes. Not unfrequently the crop is so poor that one is forced to believe that the seed-grower had drawn out all the good radishes for market, and allowed all the poor ones to run up for seed.

The method of raising radishes, above described, is not often practised by market gardeners. They think their land is too valuable, and they aim to grow them as a secondary crop. They sometimes sow the radish seed carefully and evenly, broadcast, on the asparagus bed, and sometimes they sow the seed, broadcast, on land drilled in with beets, or between the rows of early cabbages, but in the ordinary farm-garden it is best to devote the entire land to the crop. Sow the radish seed in rows, cultivate thoroughly, and by the middle of June the crop will be marketed, and the land can be plowed and used for other crops, such as Swedes turnips, beets, cabbages, etc. The best varieties of radish for home use, are the Round Scarlet Turnip, New French Breakfast, and Rose Olive-shaped. The White Turnip radish is similar to the Red Turnip, except in color. For market the Long Scarlet Short Top is one of the best varieties.

RAISING RADISH SEED.

As a rule, nearly all our radish seed is imported from Europe. It is easily grown, and as large quantities of it are annually required, it would pay any young man wonderfully well to grow radish seed, and take special pains to grow it only from the most perfect roots. The seed should be sown in rows, from twenty-one to twenty-five inches apart. The ground should be rich and clean.

Sow the best seed that can be obtained, early in the spring, dropping two or three seeds to each inch of row. Keep the ground thoroughly cultivated, and when the plants grow large enough to show their character, thin them, leaving only the handsomest and best roots. I know this is easier said than done, but it is well worth all the time and labor it will cost. It will be necessary to go over the piece several times, as it is necessary to pull out six or eight radishes for every one that is ultimately left. If we leave two or three plants for every foot of row they will be quite thick enough. Nothing more is required, except to kill the weeds, until the crop of seed is ready to harvest.

When the pods begin to wither, the crop can be cut with a sharp corn knife, or mown with a scythe, or better still, it may be cut with a self-raking reaper, which throws the stems into bundles from ten to fifteen feet apart. In our dry, hot climate, the bundles can be allowed to cure on the ground, where they are left by the reaper, turning them occasionally to prevent their moulding underneath. When thoroughly dry, draw them into the barn and stow them away on a scaffold, where the air can circulate through them, and let them remain until winter, thrashing them with a flail or thrashing machine during frosty weather.

A thrashing machine, which tears the pods to pieces, is better than a flail. The seed is easily cleaned with a fanning mill and the necessary sieves. The seed-grower should confine himself to two or three of the best varieties, and it is best for him to raise only one variety at a time. The seed retains its vitality for three years or more, and it is better to raise three acres of one variety every third year than to raise one acre each of three varieties every year. He will have just as much land in radish seed every year, but he can manage the three acres of one variety in one piece, with far less labor than he can raise an acre of each variety in three separate fields.

WINTER RADISHES.

Winter radishes are attracting considerable attention of late. They are best sown in rows, twenty-one inches apart, and cultivated with a horse-hoe. They are sown from the middle of July to the first of September. Drop the seed in the drill, three or four to each inch, and if the weather is very dry, and the ground not in the very

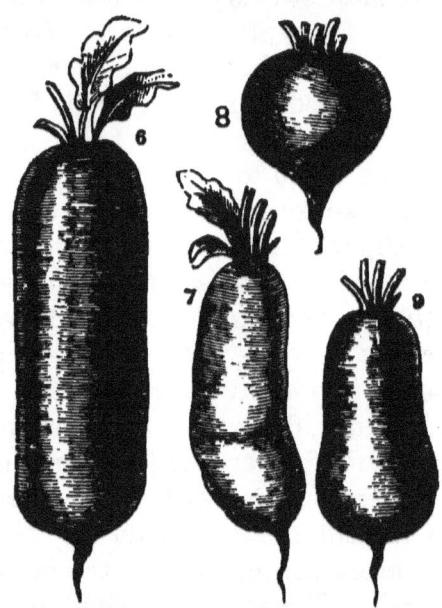

Fig. 19.—WINTER RADISHES.
6. Mammoth White Winter. 7. Chinese White Winter. 8. Black Spanish Turnip.
9. Chinese Rose Winter.

best condition, I would sow five or six seeds to each inch in hopes of securing a stand and escaping the ravages of the Black-beetle. Cultivate as soon as the rows can be distinguished, and hoe if necessary; when the plants begin to crowd each other, thin out, so as to ultimately leave them from three to four inches apart. The roots are preserved for winter use in barrels or boxes of sand in the cellar, or they can be pitted in the garden, taking the precaution to scatter among them not less than a bushel of sand or dry earth to each two or three bushels of radishes. Cover with nine inches of straw and about six inches of soil, and just before winter sets in, put on another layer of straw and cover with six inches more of soil, or enough to completely hide and cover all the straw.

The leading varieties of winter radishes are the Chinese White, the Chinese Rose, California Mammoth White, and the Black Spanish. The latter is a very hardy variety, somewhat harsh to ordinary tastes, but seems to be highly relished by those who like it. The California Mammoth White is a larger and somewhat milder variety, and would suit ordinary tastes better than the Black Spanish. The seed is grown by setting out some of the best selected roots in the spring, in rows two feet apart, and six inches distant in the row; harvest and thrash the same as directed for summer radish.

RHUBARB.

When raised from seed, Rhubarb is sown as early in the spring as the ground can be properly worked. Prepare the soil as directed for raising celery plants. Any one who can raise these well, can raise good rhubarb plants. If convenient, the seed may be sown in a box in the house, or in a moderately warm hot-bed, and the plants set out in rows twenty-one inches apart, and two to three inches apart in the row, as soon as the weather and soil will permit. The land can not be too rich, and if it is not intended to use the horse-hoe between the rows, they may be from twelve to fifteen inches apart, and kept clean by the frequent use of the hoe. When sown in the open ground, the plants need not be transplanted, but should be thinned out to three inches apart in the row. As in raising celery plants out of doors, it is impossible to make the land too rich. I have worked in well-rotted manure at the rate of one hundred two-horse loads per acre, and it pays to do so. Few people understand how much manure land will hold. An acre of soil, ten inches deep, weighs about two million pounds; if you work in one hundred tons of manure per acre, there will be only one pound of manure to ten pounds of soil; and you can put one hundred loads of manure on an acre and work it so thoroughly that one could not tell, without careful examination, that the land had been manured at all. That is the way to prepare land for raising celery and rhubarb plants. On such land, if sown as early as possible in the spring, and the plants carefully hoed and kept entirely free from weeds, the plants will be large enough to set out in their permanent bed the following spring.

Rhubarb is more generally propagated by a division of the roots, than from the seeds. When propagated from the roots, divide up the old root so as to leave one bud or crown on each piece. The roots can be set out in the permanent bed either in autumn or early in spring; the fall perhaps is the preferable time, especially in the Southern States. If the permanent bed is made from plants raised from seed, the spring is the better time. Whether made from roots or seedling plants, the permanent bed cannot be made too rich. A hundred loads of manure per acre, is none too much, and the soil should be thoroughly worked to a depth not less than ten inches. Set out the roots or plants in rows four feet apart each way; this will require two thousand seven hundred and twenty-one per acre. Make the rows straight, and set out the roots so that the crown is two or three inches below the surface. The first year no stalks should be pulled, keeping the ground thoroughly cultivated and free from weeds. A row of radishes might be sown between the rows of rhubarb, or cabbage plants, or lettuce set there, but it is better to let the rhubarb have the whole ground the first year and certainly afterwards. Some varieties of rhubarb have a disposition to throw up numerous seed stalks; these should be cut off as they appear, as they absorb much of the sap which should be used for the rapid growth of the edible stalks. The varieties of rhubarb generally grown in this country, are Linnæus, which is of good size, good quality, and early, the Victoria, which is larger and later, and of excellent quality. The Cahoon's Seedling is a late and very large variety, which was extensively sold some years ago, under the deceptive name of "Wine Plant."

SALSIFY.

Salsify, often called Vegetable Oyster, is rarely grown to perfection. When well grown and properly cooked, it is a healthful and delicious vegetable, and deserves to be much more generally and extensively cultivated. The cultivation of salsify is precisely the same as for parsnips. It is important to get good seed grown from carefully selected roots. The seed can be sown as early in the spring as the ground is in good working condition, and I have sown it as late as the first week in June with excellent results. As a rule, however, it is desirable to sow it early. The land should be prepared in the autumn, and it can not be made too deep, or too rich, and mellow. It will do well on a great variety of soils. I have had a fine crop on a well worked, heavily manured clay, but as a rule it is better to sow it on a sandy loam, heavily manured the fall previous or early in the spring. I sow in rows, twenty inches apart. The seed is long and slim, and few drills will sow it evenly without wasting the seed, and as that is quite expensive, it is better to sow it by hand, dropping about two seeds to an inch of row, and covering half an inch deep; if the weather is dry, and the soil very light, it may be covered an inch or an inch and a half, and in dry weather it is desirable to roll the soil after sowing. As soon as the plants appear, hoe lightly on each side of the row, and a few days later, run the horse-hoe or cultivator between the rows; suffer not a weed to grow, and ultimately thin out the plants, leaving them from four to six inches apart. As usually grown, the roots are quite small, because the plants are left too thick in the row. Grown as I have recommended, the crop requires considerable land, but the roots will be so large and fine, as to command an extra price, and much more than pay the extra cost of the land. Salsify is a good crop for the field-garden, where land is comparatively cheap. The roots bring the highest price in spring. Like parsnips, salsify can be left in the ground all winter; but at least a portion should be dug in the fall, and kept in pits or in the cellar, as recommended for parsnips. The seed can be grown as recommended for parsnips, though the roots may be left thicker in the row, as the stalks do not grow more than three feet high. It is well to have the rows forty-two inches apart for convenience in gathering. The seeds do not all mature at the same time, and it is usual to go over the piece two or three times and cut off the heads of seed as soon as they turn brown. There is but one variety of salsify. We must look to careful selection of roots to give us a good strain. There is an abundant opportunity for improvement in this direction, and I hope some of the boys will give us an improved salsify—not in name, but in reality. It can easily be done, by continued selection of the very best and handsomest roots for seed, rigorously rejecting all that are not perfect.

SEA KALE.

Sea Kale is a most delicious vegetable, which sooner or later will certainly be extensively cultivated in this country. It belongs to the same family as the cabbage. Its shoots only are eaten, and that only after being forced or blanched. It is a good deal of work to produce sea kale in perfection, but when properly grown, it is as tender as asparagus and as mild as cauliflower. Our climate is well adapted for its production in abundance, and of the choicest quality. When grown from seed, mark out the bed into rows three feet apart, then run a fifteen or eighteen-inch marker across the rows, and put a dozen seeds where the lines cross, and cover half an inch deep. When the plants appear, hoe, weed, and thin, leaving three or four plants in each hill.

Sea Kale is a perennial plant, and when the bed is once made, it will last for many years. It is propagated from the roots as well as from seed, and where those can be obtained, a year's time can be saved. When propagated from the roots of old plants, it is usual to cut these into lengths of two or three inches. In early spring, place the pieces in a box in the house or in the hot-bed, covering them very lightly with damp moss or light mould. As soon as they start to grow, and the weather is suitable, set out in a bed eighteen by thirty-six inches apart. No crop will be produced the first year, but the second year a few shoots can be removed without weakening the plants; the third year they will produce a full crop. The plant needs protection during the winter. A good plan is, to cover the bed or plants with leaves or manure or leaf-mould; this will protect the plants, and the shoots, as they push through this covering, will be blanched and be ready for use. If the plants are very vigorous, a greater depth of covering or blanching material will be needed.

SPINACH.

Spinach is an important crop in the garden, whether grown for home use or for market. It is of most value early in the spring, and for this purpose must be sown the autumn previous, on the richest and best land. You can not work the soil too thoroughly. The seed should be sown in rows from twelve to twenty-one inches apart, the latter distance if a horse-hoe is to be used in cultivating it. In this section we sow about the first of September, and as the ground is apt to be very dry, a good deal of work is sometimes required to break up all the clods and get the soil fine and mellow; but stick to it until the object is accomplished. By bestowing labor enough, you can get the soil into good condition. Do not wait for a rain to help you. Rain will not do much good on the hard, unbroken, or cloddy soil; but break up the land, crush the lumps, pulverize the soil, and then even a slight shower will penetrate this fine soil, and make it moist enough to start the seed. Sow the seed pretty thick, say three seeds to each inch of row; this is ten times as many as are necessary, but it is very desirable to have plants enough. Certainly it is very undesirable and annoying to have any gaps in the row. As soon as the plants appear, hoe or cultivate between the rows—the more frequently, the better. When the plants are fairly started, thin out, leaving them only four or five inches apart in the row. If desired, the plants may be thinned out with a sharp-pointed onion hoe from one to two inches apart. When large enough, half the remaining plants may be cut out for use in the fall, or just before winter sets in, at which time, and during the winter, spinach often brings a high price.

N. B.—As I said before, you can not make the land too rich for spinach. It is very desirable to work into the surface soil twenty or thirty loads of manure per acre. I would work it into the soil not more than four inches deep; but recollect it must be worked in and completely broken up, and so mixed with the soil that you would hardly know, except from the loose, mellow appearance of the land, that any manure had been applied.

Many fail in their first efforts to grow spinach in the autumn for use in spring. The reason is, they do not take sufficient pains in preparing and mellowing the land; they do not work in sufficient manure; they do not sow early enough; they do not sow seed enough; or, if the weather is dry, they do not roll the soil, or press it down hard enough after the seed is sown. In this section, just before winter sets in, it is generally desirable to scatter a thin layer of straw or horse litter over the plants, say three inches thick, as a protection. It is not always necessary, but will do no harm, and in some seasons may prevent loss.

Fig. 20.—SPINACH.

For summer use, spinach is sown in rows a foot apart, early in the spring, and again every two weeks for a succession. In warm weather it soon runs up to seed, and as we have, or may have, an abundance of other green vegetables, it is not worth while to sow spinach largely in the spring. Still, every garden should have a few rows or a small bed of it. There are two varieties commonly cultivated, the Prickly-seeded or Winter, and the Round-seeded or Summer. One is just as good as the other, either for spring or winter, and the Prickly or Winter variety should be dropped. The Round or Summer will stand the winter just as well as the Prickly, and some prefer it, thinking it is more easily sown with the drill. If sown as thickly as it ought to be sown, a good drill will sow either kind evenly and well.

SQUASH.—SUMMER.

For summer use, nearly all the varieties of Squash generally cultivated are of the bush or dwarf kind. They take up far less room in the garden than the running varieties. The cultivation of the bush squash is exceedingly simple; it requires good, but not excessively rich, land, and the seed should not be sown until the soil is quite warm and all danger of frost is passed.

In my own garden I drill in the Summer squash in rows three feet apart, dropping a seed to each two or three inches of row, and when the plants begin to crowd each other, I thin out the weakest, and leave the strongest

Fig. 21.—EARLY CROOKNECK.

and those least riddled by the Striped-bug. One good plant to each eight or ten inches of row is thick enough. Generally, however, summer squashes are planted in hills three feet one way and two feet apart in the row. Put a dozen seeds in each hill, and ultimately leave only three of the strongest plants in the hill. Keep the ground well cultivated and hoed, pulling up a little fresh soil towards the plants to smother any small weeds that can not be reached with the hoe. A tablespoonful of superphosphate, well mixed with the soil in each hill before planting the seed, stimulates the growth of the vines, and, what is still more important, it favors the early maturity of the fruit.

When grown extensively for market in the field-garden, prepare the land in the very best manner. A light, warm, sandy soil is best, but the squash will do well on heavier soil, provided it is dry and thoroughly worked until it is fine and mellow. It is seldom that such soil is worked sufficiently. Comparatively few farmers have learned how important it is to reduce soil to the finest and mellowest tilth. In the field, I would mark off the rows forty-two inches apart, and drill in the seed. I think this is better than planting in hills, but would plant in hills if more convenient. All that needs to be done is, to keep the land thoroughly cultivated with a horse-hoe between the rows, and thin out the plants in the row as previously directed.

Fig. 22.
EARLY BUSH SCOLLOP.

The best varieties of summer squash are: the Early Bush Crooknecked and the Early Bush Scollop.

SQUASH.—WINTER.

Winter squashes have running vines, and require richer land and more space than the bush varieties. They are an important crop in the field-garden. The market gardeners on high-priced land, near large cities, can rarely afford to raise winter squashes largely. They should be grown on well-prepared farm land. The fruit has not to be marketed from day to day, like summer squashes, but, like cabbages, parsnips, carrots, and potatoes, can be sent in large quantities at once to near or distant markets.

Many farmers who try to raise squashes fail to realize their expectations, simply because they do not prepare the land with sufficient care, or manure highly enough. If the land is not in the very best condition, the plants do not grow with the necessary vigor, and soon fall a prey to the remorseless Squash-bug.

Light, sandy land is best for squashes, but it should be manured either directly for the crop or for the one preceding it; in the latter case, it is desirable to manure again in the hill, thoroughly mixing the manure with the soil where the hill is to be, for a space not less than two or three square feet. Two tablespoonfuls of superphosphate to each hill, well mixed with the soil, in addition to the manure, will prove very beneficial. Plant the

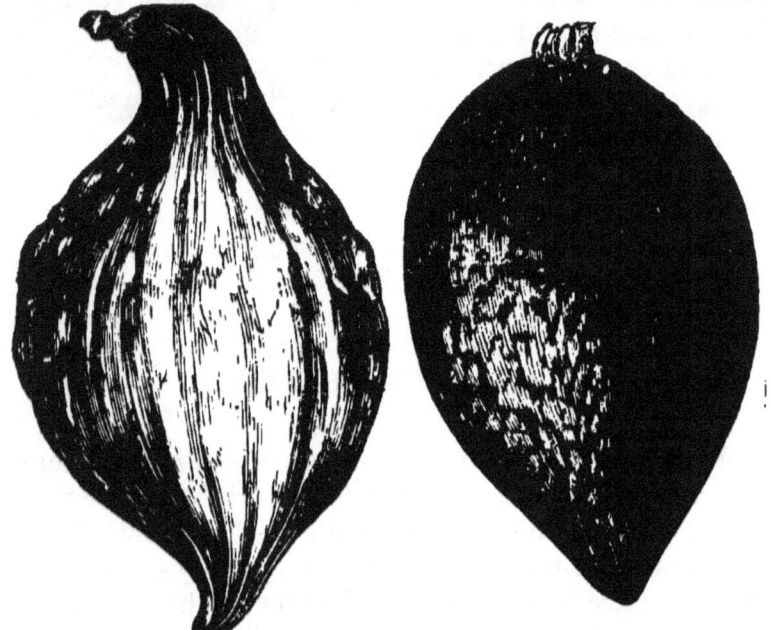

Fig. 23.—HUBBARD.   Fig. 24.—MARBLEHEAD.

squashes in rows ten feet apart, and four feet apart in the rows. Plant eight or ten seeds in each hill, and cover from one to two inches deep, according to the nature of the soil. If the weather is dry and the soil very light, cover from two to three inches deep, and make the soil all about the hill firm and smooth, with the back of the hoe. As soon as the plants begin to crack the soil, dust a little plaster over them, and in two or three days go over the piece again, early in the morning, while the dew is on, and dust on more plaster, doing the work carefully and thoroughly. The plaster is a good fertilizer for the vines and helps to keep off the bugs.

All we have to do after this, is to fight the weeds and the bugs. Not a weed should be suffered to grow. Examine the plants frequently and crush all the eggs you see on the leaves, and, as the plants begin to crowd each other, pinch off the weakest and those most injured by the bugs. If you can ultimately secure two good, strong, vigorous plants in each hill, and the land is thoroughly cultivated and free from weeds, you are almost certain of a large and profitable crop.

The best varieties for late fall and winter use are the Marblehead and Hubbard. When well grown from true seed, both are so good that it is not easy to tell which is the better. The Marblehead is quite as large as the Hubbard, the shell is a little harder and smoother; the flesh is a somewhat lighter colored, but equally dry, sweet, and fine flavored. The Hubbard is the more popular market variety.

SAVING SQUASH SEED.

No one should attempt to grow Squashes for seed unless he can keep the variety completely isolated. Where this can be done, the business is quite profitable—or at any rate it would be, as soon as the seedsmen and squash-growers became cognizant of the fact that your seed can be depended on as true to name. The main point is, to secure stock seed. I mean by this, seed that has been carefully bred for several generations. A seedsman who has such seed will not sell it, he will keep it for the exclusive purpose of raising seed.

SWEET POTATOES.

Sweet Potatoes are essentially a southern crop, and their cultivation in the Southern States is an easy and simple matter. At the North, good crops can be grown, but it is necessary to raise the plants in a greenhouse or hot-bed. Market gardeners, who grow the plants for sale, as they do tomato plants, find the business quite profitable, as there is a yearly increasing demand for the plants, which are often sent long distances by express. The plants are easily grown in the hot-bed, the chief difficulty being to preserve the potatoes intended for seed through the winter. They cannot be kept in a cool, damp cellar, like common potatoes. They should be kept in a dry room, where the thermometer never gets below forty degrees or above sixty. In this section we place the potatoes in the hot-bed, from the middle to the end of April—the cooler the bed the earlier we plant. Cut the roots lengthwise and place the cut side on the loose soil or sand in the hot-bed, and cover with sand or mould, two inches thick. As the shoots grow, more sand may be added, until it reaches the height of four or five inches above the potatoes. The shoots or young plants can be removed and set out in another hot-bed, as the potatoes will continue to throw up new shoots. In this way a large number of plants can be obtained from each. Of course, it is necessary to attend to ventilating and watering the hot-bed. The hotter the bed, and the brighter the sun, the more water will be needed. In no case must the bed be allowed to get dry. It is also necessary to guard against chilling the plants by saturating the bed with cold water. Sweet potato plants are set out in the open ground from the first of June to the first of July. A warm, sandy soil is best. It is not necessary to have the land excessively rich, or the quality of the potatoes may be injured. It is very important, however, to make the ground as mellow and loose as possible, and to keep the plants entirely free from weeds. Plant in rows forty-two inches apart and twenty-four inches apart in the row. Or plant in hills, three feet apart each way. A tablespoonful of superphosphate to each hill, mixed with the soil at the time the potato plants are set out, will favor the ripening of the crop, and improve the quality. The cultivation is similar to that required for the common, or as the southerners call it, the "Irish" potato. In damp, growing weather, the vines lying on the ground throw out roots, and it is best to check this tendency by occasionally moving the vines. If you keep working about the vines as much as is desirable with the hoe to destroy weeds, and give the plants a little fresh soil, nothing more will usually be required.

The variety generally cultivated at the North is the Nansemond.

TOMATOES.

For home use people generally depend on buying Tomato plants rather than to be at the trouble of raising them themselves. So far as this single crop is concerned, the plan is a good one, but there are plants which are all the better for being started in a hotbed or in boxes in the house, and the more of these things you have to attend to, the less likely will you be to neglect them. I would, therefore, recommend all young gardeners to raise their own tomato plants. And all the more so because, should they fail, they can readily buy plants. If they succeed in raising the plants, all the better. If they fail, none the worse. You can raise far better plants than are generally to be found in the market.

One box such as I have described, and which will fit into the window, will start all the tomato plants likely to be wanted for home use. Here we usually sow the seed the last of March or the first of April. We sow them in rows about an inch apart, and put three or four seeds to an inch of row, cover a quarter of an inch deep with a a mixture of sand and sifted moss, or moss alone. Keep the soil moderately moist, but be careful not to get it too wet. If, at the time of sowing, you saturate the soil with warm water, as good a rule as any I can give in regard to the amount of water afterwards required, is never to let the surface soil get dry. If you keep the surface soil or moss on top of the seed so moist that it will adhere together, that will be sufficient. Until the plants grow, very little water will be required, but that little should be given every day. It should be milk warm, or about as warm as your hand, and be sprinkled on with a fine rose. If any weeds appear, pull them out. And as soon as the plants begin to crowd, some of them should be removed into another box. As soon as the plants begin to crowd, transplant them again into a spent hotbed or cold frame, covered with glass or muslin. There they can remain until the soil and weather will allow of their being set out in the garden.

If you have pots it is a great advantage to set a tomato plant in a three or four-inch pot and plunge the pots in the soil of a moderately warm hot-bed. If the plants get too large before the ground is ready for them in the garden, transfer them, soil and all, to a pot of larger size, and throw fresh soil into the pot to fill the space. Press the soil in firm, and put in enough to fill the pot, the roots will soon fill it, and you will have strong, healthy, stocky plants, each one of which is worth a dozen of the lank, crowded plants sometimes offered for sale.

The preparation of the soil in the garden for tomato

plants needs careful attention. It does not need to be specially rich, but it must be made as fine and mellow as the most thorough working with the plow or spade and hoe and rake can secure. The soil should never be worked when wet. The dryer it is the lighter you can make it, and the lighter it is the warmer and better will it be for tomatoes. In setting out the tomato plants be very careful to press this dry, light soil firmly round their roots. If the plants are in pots, transplanting is a safe and easy matter, though an important one. Before transplanting saturate the soil in the pots with water, nearly milk warm. The best way to do this is to place the pots containing the tomatoes in a wash-tub or shallow box, containing water enough to nearly cover them. Let them remain in the water at least four or five minutes, then remove them and let them drain for an hour or so, or until you are ready to set them out.

Plant in rows four feet apart, and not less than two feet apart in the rows. Set a line (and be sure you do not forget this), as crooked rows should never be tolerated in the garden; make holes with a hoe where the plants are to be set, and if you work into the soil about a tablespoonful of superphosphate it will be very beneficial. Then, every thing being ready, place your two fingers on each side of the plant, reverse the pot so that the plant will hang down and strike the edge of the pot on any hard substance which happens to be handy, say the top of a spade, or the side of the wheelbarrow, or the top of the wooden pail containing the superphosphate. Set the plant, with the ball of moist earth, undisturbed, into the hole, so deep that the surface of the soil will be fully up to the first leaves of the plant, pull the soil to, and press it firmly around the roots of the plant with the hands, and the work is done. And if well done, you have every reason to expect a grand crop of tomatoes. Do not waste your time in watering the plants, it is unnecessary and useless; the moist soil which was around the roots when taken out of the pot, will furnish all the moisture needed. In setting out tomato plants from a box or hot-bed, the soil should be prepared as before directed. The plants in the boxes or hot-bed should have the soil thoroughly saturated with warm water. I mean by that, you should put on as much water as the soil will hold. And recollect that soil will hold a great deal more water than most people would suppose. A good garden soil will hold from fifty to seventy-five per cent. of its weight of water. Such soil or mould as we use in the hot-bed, or for potting plants, will hold its own weight of water; in other words, if you have a pot containing two pounds of saturated mould, one pound of it will be water. I mention this to show that when you undertake to water a sash full of tomato plants in the hot-bed before transplanting them, it will take a good deal of water, and you will be very apt to get tired before you have put on all that the soil will hold. There is no danger of putting on too much, for after the earth is saturated it will hold no more, but the excess will soak into the manure below. The better way is, to do the work of watering the night before you intend to set out the plants. While the plants are growing, water should always be applied through a rose, but now that you intend to remove them from the hot-bed, this is not necessary; it will facilitate the work if you will take a small garden fork and break up the soil between the rows of plants; you can then take off the rose from the watering pot, and pour on the water as fast as the soil will absorb it. Next morning break up the soil again with the fork, and take up each plant by putting your fingers on both sides of it and squeezing a ball of the loose, wet soil, around the roots. On no account pull up the plants, as this will break off many of the fine roots. Set out the plants, with this ball of moist earth around the roots, down to the first leaves, and press the soil firmly around the ball of moist earth. It ought not to be necessary to water the plants after setting out, but if the sun is very hot, a piece of newspaper,

Fig. 25.—VARIETIES OF THE TOMATO. 1. Red Cherry. 2. Persian Yellow. 3. Hathaway's Excelsior. 4. General Grant. 5. Early Smooth Red. 6. Hubbard's Curled Leaf.

a foot or eighteen inches square, may be placed over each plant; this will shade them and check the evaporation of water from the leaves. The plants will in any case be apt to wilt a little, but this will not hurt them.

The after-cultivation of tomatoes is usually of the simplest kind. I say usually, because sometimes, in the garden, tomatoes are trained to a trellis two and one-half or three feet high. By a little judicious training and pruning, they are quite ornamental, and produce very fine fruit. But in our dry climate, tomatoes are seldom injured by allowing the vines to trail on the ground; and after setting out the plants, all that the tomato-grower need do is to keep the ground well stirred up and clean, by the frequent use of the cultivator and hoe.

Tomatoes are now largely grown for the canning establishments. The profit of the crop, however, depends on our ability to get early fruit and market it for consumption, while it brings the highest price. Early in the season you can generally get a dollar a basket for the first tomatoes, while, as the season advances and the crop becomes more abundant, the price falls to sixty, fifty, or forty cents per bushel, and sometimes in September, they are sold for ten cents per basket. A basket of tomatoes weighs about thirty pounds, or sixty-six baskets to the ton. The canning establishments pay from eight to fifteen dollars per ton, or at the rate of from twelve and one-half to twenty-three cents per basket. If the whole crop was sold to the canning establishments, the profit would be very moderate; but taken in connection with the high price obtained for the early fruit, twenty cents per basket does very well, and is more profitable than ordinary farm crops. But in this, as in all other crops, a great deal depends on securing a large yield per acre. This depends on the length of the season and the power of the sun to ripen the fruit. If the land is rich and is kept well cultivated, and entirely free from weeds, a hot, dry season is favorable. Sixteen tons per acre, or one thousand baskets may be considered a maximum crop.

The best varieties for the general crop, are Hathaway's

Excelsior, Acme, Trophy, and General Grant. The earliest variety is the Hubbard Curled Leaf, but it should be planted only to a limited extent, as it is small and not of the best quality. It is only good until we can get something better. In the cool summer of 1882, when many of the later varieties failed to ripen, we had an excellent crop from Hubbard Curled Leaf. I never knew it do so well or produce such an abundant crop of fine fruit before. The Early Smooth Red is still a favorite in many sections. Persian Yellow is a large tomato of a creamy yellow color. The Red Cherry is a small variety grown for pickling and preserving.

TOMATOES FOR SEED.

It is not an easy matter to get really good, well-bred tomato seed, and I would advise some of my young friends to make a speciality of growing it. The entire crop should be devoted to the one object of growing the choicest and best seed, and that only. It will not do to market or eat the earliest and best fruit, and then save the seed from what is left. Every plant that does not prove true to kind, should be remorselessly and promptly pulled up and thrown away; by continuing this careful selection for a few years, such a tomato-grower would find a good demand for all the seed he could produce at remunerative prices. At first it might not pay him, as he might have to sell the seed for the same price as common seed. Tomato seed retains its vitality six or seven years, and it would be well for the seed-grower to save the seed of only one variety each year.

To extract the seed, mash the tomatoes, throw them into a barrel with water, and allow them to ferment; the seed will fall to the bottom, and the scum rise to the top, when it can be skimmed off. I generally throw the skimmings into another barrel and allow them to ferment twenty-four or forty-eight hours longer; the seed can be allowed to remain in the fermenting barrel for several days without injury to its germinating powers, but it does not look quite so bright as that first taken from the barrel after it has been allowed to ferment thirty-six or forty-eight hours. It is convenient to have plenty of barrels and an abundance of water. A little knowledge of chemistry, with some experience, will greatly facilitate the labor of washing out and drying the seed. It will facilitate the drying process if you press out as much water as possible, either by squeezing the seeds between the hands or putting them in a bag under a cheese press, before putting them on the stretchers to dry. The seed must be thoroughly dried before being bagged and stowed away.

TURNIPS.

The cultivation of Turnips merely for home use, as a table vegetable, will not require much thought or labor. But when grown extensively either as a farm crop for stock, or as a farm-garden crop for market, it will be necessary to bestow considerable attention upon them. It is often thought that our climate is not well adapted to the growth of turnips. I am satisfied that this is a mistake. We can grow just as good turnips here, and as large a crop per acre, as in any other country. The reason probably why the English and Scotch farmers raise turnips so extensively, is not that they can grow them so much better or more easily than we can, but because their winters are so much milder, that the roots can be largely eaten off by sheep during the autumn, winter and spring months on the land where they grow. If an English farmer could sell his turnips at any thing like the price the crop will bring in this country, no other farm crop would be half so profitable. But, as I said before, this is not because the climate is any better than our own for the production of the crop, but because long experience has enabled British farmers to use the very best methods in its cultivation. I have known an English farmer to spend fifty dollars an acre in preparing his land for turnips. It should be understood that turnips can not be grown with the preparation of the land necessary for corn and potatoes.

Turnip seed is small, and it is useless to sow it among clods and expect it to germinate. The land for turnips must be in the very best possible condition. If it is necessary to plow it twice, plow it twice; if three times are necessary, then plow it three times. Either abandon the idea of raising the crop, or work the land and keep working it, until not a clod or hard spot remains. Superphosphate of lime is confessedly the best of all artificial fertilizers for turnips; and now that it is so easily obtained, and at such a reasonable price, there is no reason why turnips should not be more extensively grown. In the market turnips usually bring very liberal prices, and the crop has this advantage, if it can not be sold in market, it can be fed out on the farm. Horses are very fond of ruta-bagas, or sweet turnips. I do not say that they are a better or cheaper food for them in this country than corn or oats, but after your horse has had the usual allowance of oats or corn, he will not be sorry when the price of ruta-bagas falls so low in market that you will not begrudge him three or four good-sized roots every day.

Ruta-bagas or Swedes usually pay better than the early white-fleshed varieties. But I should perhaps here say that turnips may be divided into three classes. One class is well represented by the common Strap-leaf variety; it is sown late in the summer, and grows with the greatest rapidity; but it is not a good keeper, which is true of all of this class. These are grown very extensively in England to be eaten on the land by sheep in October and November; they grow quickly, but contain comparatively little nutriment. I have known a large crop that grew very rapidly to contain ninety-five per cent. of water; in other words, one ton of the turnips contained only one hundred pounds of real food. An animal eating such turnips, has therefore to take in nineteen pounds of water to get one pound of real food; no wonder such turnips can grow rapidly, and no wonder they will not keep long.

The second class, of which the Yellow Aberdeen and Yellowstone are good examples, requires to be sown earlier. They will grow larger and keep later than those of the first class.

Class third includes all the varieties known as Swede turnips, or Ruta-bagas, they are essentially winter varieties. They must be sown earlier than the other classes, and require richer land; they are far more nutritious than the others, and will keep late into the following spring. I wish this matter to be understood. People often ask for the best variety of turnips; they might just as well ask for the best variety of apples. If you ask which is the best summer apple, the best early or late autumn apple, or which is the best winter apple, an experienced fruit-grower might be able to answer the question. And so it is with turnips, we have early and late autumn kinds, and winter or early spring kinds; the latter class being Ruta-bagas or Swede turnips.

Fig. 26.
IMPERIAL PURPLE TOP SWEDE.

The cultivation of such varieties as the Strap-leaf is often no cultivation at all. The seed is scattered on any vacant spot, from the middle of July to the first of September, and we trust to chance for a crop. One year in five we get a good crop; one year in three we get a fair crop, on perhaps one-fourth of the land, while on three-fourths of the field the turnips are not worth gathering. I do not say that it does not pay to sow turnips in this way; very little labor is required, the land would otherwise lie idle, and one pound of seed is amply sufficient to sow an acre; in fact, if you can distribute it evenly, half a pound is enough. It is quite a knack to sow turnip seed broadcast; all the seed required is what you can hold between your thumb and the first two fingers; scatter the seed over a width of about ten feet, then take two steps forward and throw another similar pinch; throw it boldly, and keep your hand all the time on a level with your shoulder; most people let their hand fall as low as the hip, but the other is far the better way; it insures a much more even distribution of the seed. But I do not want my young friends to be sowing turnips broadcast. As a rule, what is worth doing at all is worth doing well. And now that we have the best of implements to prepare the land, good drills to sow the seed, and good hoes to thin out the plants, I am very confident that, taking one year with another, it is far more profitable to drill in turnip seed, and cultivate between the rows with a horse-hoe than it is to sow broadcast. It is not merely that you get two or three, or four times as many bushels of turnips per acre, but you are almost certain of a crop, even in the most unfavorable season. When a good crop is obtained from sowing broadcast, and leaving the plants to take care of themselves, the market will be glutted with turnips, and the price will be low; but in an ordinary season, when you will not get more than half a crop from the broadcast sowing, on half the land, turnips will command a good price, and the farmer or gardener who has a good crop, gets ample compensation for his enterprise and labor; while the very next year, the season may be so unfavorable that the broadcast turnips are almost a universal failure, and the good cultivator who has a good crop, can sell turnips enough from an acre of land to buy him a horse and buggy. Let us then abandon the idea of sowing turnips broadcast, except in rare cases.

CULTIVATION OF RUTA-BAGAS.

Ruta-bagas, or Swede Turnips—or as it would be better to call them, Winter Turnips, should be sown about corn-planting time, or from that until about the time we usually plant beans. I have myself had a good crop sown as late as July 4th, but from the last of May to the middle of June is the better time in this section.

Land that will raise good corn will produce good turnips, but ruta-bagas do better on a somewhat stiff loam than on a light sandy one; they will do very well on sandy soil provided you make it rich enough. On the stiff soils, it is better to prepare the land the autumn previous. If the land has been in corn or potatoes, plow it as soon as the crop is removed; the earlier the better; harrow, roll, and pick up and draw off all stones large enough to interfere with a cultivator. If the land is at all weedy, plow or cultivate, and harrow and roll during dry weather in autumn, until all the weeds are killed. If the work has been well done, this thorough cultivation will start into growth millions of weed seeds. Before cold weather sets in, plow the land again, and leave it rough for the winter. The frost will break up the stiff lumps of clay, and the next spring they will readily crumble to pieces, and produce the very best soil for ruta-bagas. Do not plow the land in the spring until it is quite dry; the surface may bake, but when you come to plow it, you will find that the soil underneath will turn up fine, mellow, and moist.

If barn-yard manure is to be used, there are two methods of applying it; one plan is to spread it broadcast all over the land, and another, to make ridges or furrows, thirty inches apart and put the manure in these furrows, carefully knocking it to pieces with the fork or hoe. Cover up the manure by splitting the ridges with the plow. A double mould-board plow does the work twice as fast as a common plow, and in skillful hands does it far better. The turnip seed is then drilled in on these ridges, immediately above the manure. To do the work expeditiously and well, not only a good double mould-board plow is required, but a turnip drill with a roller before and behind the coulter which deposits the seed.

Without these implements and more or less skill in their use, a young turnip-grower had better apply his manure broadcast, and after the land is thoroughly prepared, drill in the seed on the flat surface. He need not regret the necessity for adopting this method, for it is not without some advantages over the other. In ridging and applying the manure between the ridges, you must make the furrows wide enough apart to allow the wheels of the wagon or cart to go in them.

In other words you will have to make the ridges about thirty inches apart, which is wider than it is necessary to drill in the turnips. I find no difficulty, with a steady horse, of running a cultivator between rows of turnips or beets twenty-one inches apart, and if your land is rich enough, you can grow a far larger crop in these close rows than you can in wide ones. I think, however, it will usually be better to have the rows two feet apart, and to thin the turnips to ten or twelve inches in the rows.

If the rows are two feet apart, and the plants one foot in the row, we have twenty-one thousand seven hundred and eighty plants on an acre. If the rows are thirty inches apart, and the plants a foot apart in the rows, we have seventeen thousand four hundred and twenty-four plants on an acre. If the turnips average four pounds each, the one crop on the ridges would give us less than thirty-five tons per acre, while the crop on the flat, in the narrow rows, would give us over forty-three tons per acre, or reckoning the turnips at sixty pounds per bushel, the crop on the narrow rows would give us one thousand four hundred and fifty-two bushels to the acre, while in the wider rows the crop would be less than one thousand one hundred and ninety-two bushels to the acre.

I am free to admit, that either crop would be a remarkably good one, but I am advocating good cultivation and the liberal use of fertilizers. During the winter of 1881—'82, it would have been a very easy matter to have disposed of thousands of bushels of ruta-bagas at fifty cents a bushel, and even one thousand bushels per acre would have afforded a magnificent profit.

But before you can make a profit of five hundred dollars an acre from a crop of turnips, you have something to do. I speak of these prospective and possible profits as an incentive to faith, hope, and labor. I want you to have faith in good farming, and not be afraid to put work and manure into the land. There are some drawbacks and difficulties and many seeming discouragements; there are drouths, Black-beetles, Turnip-lice and mildew, but if there were none of these, turnips would never bring fifty cents a bushel. The best remedies for all of these is, the thorough preparation of the land, liberal manuring and frequent cultivation between the rows of plants, and careful thinning out and hoeing in the rows.

If flat cultivation is adopted and the land is prepared in the autumn, as previously recommended, the manure may be spread on the land in the spring before plowing; though I think it is better to plow the land first. My own plan is, to draw the manure to the field during the winter and put it in large square heaps, about five feet high; in the spring, if necessary, turn over the heaps to facilitate decomposition.

When the manure is in heaps in the field, it is an easy matter to draw it about the lot, even if the land has been plowed; put it in rows about five yards apart, and make the heaps at about the same distance in rows. This would give one hundred and ninety-three heaps on an acre, and if you put three bushels of manure in each heap, and each bushel weighs seventy-five pounds, you would put on a little over twenty tons to the acre. If the manure is good, and you apply three or four hundred pounds of superphosphate per acre in addition, this amount will be amply sufficient to produce a grand crop of turnips.

Spread the manure evenly on the land, and then go over it with a smoothing harrow lengthwise, and crosswise of the furrows two or three times, until the manure is thoroughly broken up and mixed with the soil. Not a single lump should remain visible. This is an important matter, and you should do the work very thoroughly. If you are inclined to shrink from the labor and expense, think of a thousand bushels of turnips to the acre, and what they are likely to be worth in market, and go over the land once more with a harrow.

The next step depends on the nature of the soil. My own soil varies greatly. I have in the same field a black sand, with more or less muck in it, and a sandy knoll with a stiff, tenacious loam between. It is not necessary to plow the muck or the dry sand as much as the heavier soil. And yet, as a matter of fact, the light soil is always better plowed than the other, as the plow goes in deeper than it does on the clay. I find it better to plow the heavier soil by itself, even if it is necessary to turn round every few rods. When thoroughly reduced by good and repeated plowing, the heavier soil gives the best crops, but if carelessly plowed, with a point good enough to go in on the sand, but which skims over the dry, hard clayey spots, we should be pretty certain to get no crop worth harvesting. As I cannot tell the kind of land on which you are going to sow the turnips, I cannot tell you just how to work it; it is one of the advantages of agriculture and horticulture, that each man must do his own thinking. All I can say is this: for turnips, the land must be worked with a plow, the gang-plow, the cultivator, the harrow and the roller, until not a lump remains on the surface or within reach of the drill.

Before the last harrowing and rolling, or earlier, sow on the superphosphate at the rate of three hundred pounds per acre; be careful to distribute it evenly, and if the superphosphate is not entirely free from lumps, run it through a sieve and break them up fine; go over the land once more with the smoothing harrow or roller; set a line—do not forget this—and drill in the seed, in rows two feet apart. The drill makes its own mark, but if you find the rows are getting crooked, set the line again, and in such a way that in no point it shall be less than two feet from the last drill mark. If the soil is moist, the shallower you can sow the seed the better, provided it is covered at all; but if the surface-soil is dry, you may set the drill to deposit the seed half an inch deep, or until it will reach the moist soil below. I would sow at least two seeds to each inch of row, and if the soil is dry, with little prospect of rain, I would sow three or four seeds to each inch of row, or two pounds to the acre. If the soil and weather are moist, and every thing is favorable, one pound is sufficient; but in average conditions two pounds per acre is the rule. It is better to sow three, four, or even five pounds per acre, than to run any risk of losing your crop by the swarms of black beetles which frequently attack the young plants. After the turnip plants get into the rough leaf, the beetles do them comparatively little harm. As soon, therefore, as the plants get into the rough leaf, commence to hoe and thin them out. Hoeing turnips and thinning them out, are both done at the same time. You may think the remark unnecessary, but I have known people to hoe on each side of the row of turnips and afterwards go over the piece and thin them out. The true plan is, to cultivate the turnips between the rows with a horse-hoe, that will pull a little soil away from the row. If the rows are straight, a skillful boy will run his cultivator within an inch of the plants; when through cultivating, the young turnip plants will stand in straight rows two inches in width, invitingly ready for the hoe.

Have the hoe ground sharp and bright, square at the corners, with the shank bent at nearly right angles with the handle; then dash your hoe boldly across the row of turnips, pulling it towards you; then push it back slowly in such a way as to leave only one plant in a place. The work can nearly all be done with a hoe, but occasionally, when the plants interlock, it will be necessary to stoop down and remove all but one with the thumb and finger. For this reason, if the plants are very thick in the row, you must commence to single out as early as possible, and push forward the work with energy. It will not do to loiter or tell stories. If you do, the plants will assuredly get the start of you, and then you have a tough job on hand. If, in spite of all you can do, you find you can not get through the whole piece before the plants are likely to be injured by over crowding, the better way is, to go through the whole piece and bunch out the plants. By this I mean strike the hoe across the row, leaving bunches of plants ten or twelve inches apart, and afterwards go over them again and single them out.

Turnips will stand rougher treatment than beets or mangels. If you cut too close to a beet plant, our hot sun will kill it; while a turnip in the same circumstances would revive during the next night. After the plants are singled our for the first time, all that you have to do is, to keep the cultivator frequently running between the rows. As soon as any weeds appear among the turnips, that can not be reached by the cultivator, go over the piece again with the hoe, and cut out all the weeds, and at the same time single out any plants that may have been left double, and this is all that will be necessary until the crop is ready to harvest.

GATHERING THE CROP.

Ruta-bagas, or Winter Turnips, will stand quite a sharp frost without injury, especially if at the time the frost occurs, the roots are surmounted by an abundance of green vigorous leaves. As long, therefore, as the leaves of the turnips keep green, there is no particular necessity for pulling up the crop; as the great difficulty in keeping turnips in large piles or pits, during the winter, is their tendency to heat—the colder the weather, provided the roots are not actually frozen when the crop is gathered, the better will the roots keep. If the crop is in by Thanksgiving Day, it will be early enough three seasons out of four. My own plan is, to pit the roots in the field as we do potatoes and mangels. We plow out a wide, deep, dead-furrow. We mark out the spot where the pit is to be, of any desired length, and then measure off six or eight feet on each side, and start the plow, plowing up and down on both sides, until the center, or dead-furrow is reached; then commence on the outside again, and plow up and down as before. This will make a still deeper and wider dead-furrow; then commence on the outside again, and plow up and down again as before, plowing deeper as you approach the center. These three plowings will give a mass of deep, mellow earth, which will afterwards be very convenient for covering the pit.

It will also bid defiance to the severest frost. If necessary, the bottom of this wide, deep, dead-furrow, may be cleaned out and made flat, level, and square with the spade or shovel; the pit is then ready for the roots. No straw is needed at the bottom or sides. The days are short, winter is approaching, and you must work lively and make a short job of it.

My plan is, to set three teams with stone-boats to drawing the untopped turnips to the pit; one man, with the team and stone-boat, takes two rows at a time, and as soon as he has put on all he can carry, he drives to the pit, where a couple of men help him to top the turnips and throw them into the pit. By the time this is done, another load is at the pit, and the empty stone-boat goes for another load, and by the time the second load is topped, the third team is at the pit with a load waiting to be topped. If all hands work sharp, a great lot of turnips can be gathered, topped, and pitted in a day. On my own farm, I generally find it best to have an extra man to help the drivers to pull and load the turnips; if both work well, this doubles the speed of the whole operation. In other words, we have two men pulling turnips all the time, and two men ought to pull twice as many as one man. In fact, I have sometimes thought that two good sharp boys would pull more than twice as many turnips as one man who spends one-third of his time in stopping and starting the team. Two active boys, who work during these short days with a will, can pull up two rows of turnips and put them on the stone-boat almost as fast as a slow team will walk. If they cannot top the turnips fast enough at the pit, put on another man, or what is better still, take hold and help yourself. As a rule, however, the man or boy who has charge of the job, should not undertake any part of the work that will occupy all his time; he had better undertake the general supervision, and be ready to lend a helping hand where most needed. There is always plenty of work to be done at the pit.

When the roots in the pit reach the level of the ground, it will be necessary to take a little more pains in placing them in it. And I would especially recommend you, if possible, to throw a quantity of dry sand or earth on the turnips in the pit. Those below the surface of the ground do not need it so much, but the turnips in the pit above the surface, and especially as they approach the top, will keep far better and fresher, if dry earth or sand is freely scattered among them. A bushel of sand to each three or four bushels of turnips will be exceedingly beneficial. I do not mean that you should draw sand from a distance, but take that which has been plowed out of the pit, giving preference to that which is driest. Do not be afraid of using too much. The sand will not only keep the turnips fresher, but it is quite a convenience in enabling you to build up the sides of the pit straighter and narrower. A wide pit is objectionable; four feet wide at the surface of the ground, and gradually tapering up to the top, to the height of three and a half to four feet, is quite large enough. It is generally recommended to place chimneys every four or five feet in the pit, for the purpose of carrying off the heat or steam. These chimneys can be made by placing a bunch of straw a foot deep among the turnips, and letting it project through the covering of earth on top. Drain tiles two or three inches in diameter are equally effective.

If the work is delayed until just before winter sets in, and the turnips are very cold when put in the pit, and above all, if plenty of dry sand has been mixed with the roots, and a liberal coat of straw, say six or eight inches thick, is placed on top of the roots from the surface to the apex, there is very little danger that the turnips will get too hot in the pit. As I have said before, this is the real difficulty in keeping turnips. It is a very easy matter to keep out the frost. When the pit is finished, get a load of dry straw and cover the pit evenly all over, six or eight inches thick, and at the same time commence to cover it with earth, working from the surface of the land upwards. If, in doing this, you find any part where the straw is too thin, add more straw. Just earth enough to hide the straw should be put on. Make the surface of the soil smooth, so that it will readily shed rain, and the work is done for the present.

Later, however, it may be necessary to give the pit another covering of straw and earth, and before it is left, plow around it half a dozen times, to the width of five or six feet on both sides of the pit, turning the furrows towards the pit. This is very important. You cannot plow too much or too deeply, as loose earth is an excellent non-conductor of heat, and the severest frost will do little more in any single night than crust over the surface of this repeatedly plowed land. When cold weather really sets in, plow around the heap again, two or three times; put on a thin layer of straw, say four or five inches thick, and cover with the loose soil thrown up by the plow. You will find that the plow, properly handled, will save more than half the labor, and what is better still, the work is likely to be more thoroughly done.

This last covering should be delayed until cold weather sets in, and it is all the better if the first coat of earth on the pit is frozen solid. I have more than once put on this second covering during a severe storm, with the thermometer almost down to zero. I once had to work with every man and team on the farm to help until ten o'clock at night to cover my pits, so suddenly and savagely came on the storm. We had to keep the teams plowing rapidly around the pits to furnish loose unfrozen soil. There was no let-up for many weeks. Had we not done this, the loss would have been very great; as it was, not a root or potato was injured. I do not advocate delaying the work quite so late as this, but if you get caught, do not hesitate to work during the storm. If you do the work well, you can go to sleep afterwards, with a consciousness that, no matter how the storm may rage, your root crops are entirely safe.

The method of keeping turnips here recommended is generally adapted to keeping beets, mangels, carrots, parsnips, etc.

FALL, OR EARLY WINTER TURNIPS.

As a rule, this intermediate class of turnips has attracted very little attention in this country. It would not at present be advisable to raise them largely. I should not raise them at all, unless I had land all ready for the crop the first or second week in July, when it was too late to be sure of getting a crop of ruta-bagas. In a case like this, such varieties as the Yellow Aberdeen can be sown from the middle of July to the first of August with great advantage; you can get a large crop to the acre; far greater than you can of the Strap-leaf, Flat Dutch and other early varieties sown later. The Yellow Aberdeen will keep in excellent condition from December to February, and be valuable for the table, when the early varieties have become pithy and tasteless. When better known, it will prove a profitable variety for the market garden, as it has always been for the stock feeder. The cultivation of the Yellow Aberdeen and similar varieties, does not differ essentially from that of the ruta-bagas; it does not need to be sown so early, and does not require so rich land. A soil in good mechanical condition, that has been liberally manured for the previous crop, will, by the aid of a dressing of three hundred pounds per acre of superphosphate sown broadcast, produce a fine crop without any other manure; but if the land has not been manured for the previous crop, it will be better to give it a moderate dressing of manure, say eight tons per acre, and use the superphosphate in addition. Superphosphate cannot be applied to any crop where it will do more good than to turnips.

The Aberdeen is a hardy variety and will stand considerable frost, but it should be gathered before the ruta-bagas. In other words, you can let ruta-bagas remain later in the field than you can the Yellow Aberdeens; they will not keep quite so well as the ruta-bagas, as they contain more water and are more liable to get heated

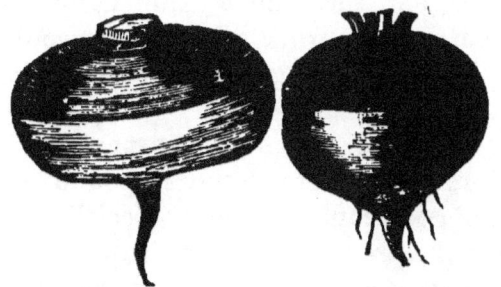

Fig. 27. Fig. 28.
PURPLE TOP STRAP-LEAF. WHITE FLAT DUTCH.

in the pit. It is better therefore to make the pit smaller and to throw in more dry earth among the roots.

CULTIVATION OF AUTUMN TURNIPS.

This class of turnips, of which the Purple Top Strap-leaf is a popular variety, is usually grown with little or no cultivation properly so called. In England, they are often called Stubble Turnips, because they can be grown after a crop of rye, wheat, or barley is harvested.

We can do the same thing here, but our climate is so much hotter and dryer, that we shall have to take considerable pains to get land from which a grain crop has just been harvested, sufficiently moist and mellow to insure the germination of turnip seed. There are times, however, when it can be done, and done to great advantage. Land should be plowed immediately after harvest, and the roller should follow the plow. You cannot roll it too much while dry; follow the roller a few days later with a smoothing harrow, weighted until it will cut through the dry clods, follow with a roller, so as to break up or crush the clods brought to the surface by the harrow, continue to roll and harrow, until you have secured a fine tilth. If the weather reporter would send us some rain, if nothing more than a thunder shower, we should at this time accept it as a favor; this thoroughly worked, but dusty soil would drink it in, and we could immediately start the drill, feeling confident that in two or three days the turnips would be up.

Do not forget to sow superphosphate at the rate of from two hundred to three hundred pounds per acre. If the land is in good condition, and especially if it has been manured for the previous crop, the superphosphate is all that is necessary. It is better to sow the phosphate previous to rolling and harrowing, but it is not well, I think, to plow it under. At this dry season of the year, it is well to roll the land after drilling in the seed and to roll it thoroughly.

I would drill in the turnips in rows not less than two feet apart, and drop at least four seeds to each inch of row, or, say from three to four pounds per acre; if the land is in good condition, this thick seeding is almost certain, with the aid of superphosphate, to enable the plants to escape the ravages of the beetle.

The cultivation is similar to that previously recommended for ruta-bagas, except that we leave the plants a little thicker in the row—say seven inches apart. If the plants are properly singled out to this distance and the cultivator is used between the rows as often as is necessary, nothing more will be required until the crop is ready to be pulled.

The sooner the crop is marketed, the better. At the price usually obtained for them, these turnips are quite profitable. It is not at all a difficult matter to grow from four hundred to five hundred bushels per acre.

SWEET HERBS.

Little need to be said in regard to the cultivation of Sweet Herbs. With the exception of Sage and Thyme, they are not very extensively grown for market.

SAGE.

Sage is grown more extensively for market than any other sweet herb. It is called Sage because its use was supposed to strengthen the memory and make people sage, or wise.

It is used extensively for seasoning or flavoring sausages, the stuffing of ducks, geese, etc., and occasionally for flavoring cheese.

The plants can be propagated by cuttings, precisely as we propagate currants, but the usual and better way is, to grow it from seed. If you have good seed, it is an easy matter to raise the plants. For some reason, however, Sage seed is often very poor and should be carefully tested before sowing. There is no difficulty whatever in growing good seed.

If you wish only a few plants for your own use, sow a paper of seed in a box in the house, the middle of March, in rows two inches apart and two seeds to each inch of row. Transplant out of doors as soon as the weather is warm and settled.

The seed, however, can be sown out of doors in the spring, as soon as the soil is in good condition. It is best to prepare the soil the fall previous. A light, warm, sandy soil in a sheltered spot, with a sunny exposure is best. Sow the seed in rows wide enough apart to admit the use of the hoe, putting in two seeds to each inch; cover the seed a quarter of an inch deep, and if the soil is dry, pat it down with the back of the spade. As soon as the plants appear, hoe lightly between the rows and keep the bed free from weeds. This is all that need be done until the plants are ready to set out where they are to grow.

The land for Sage should be dry, loose, and very rich. The plants are small and grow slowly at first. Before taking them out of the seed-bed, the soil should be deeply and carefully broken up with a fork, six or eight inches deep, and the bed thoroughly watered until all the soil to the depth of the sage roots is completely saturated. It requires a good deal of water, but if the work is well done, the young sage plants can be set out even in the hottest weather, and on comparatively dry soil, without the loss of a single plant.

It is, however, very desirable to make the land very fine and moist, by thorough cultivation. It will usually be found better to plow the land just before setting out the plants, as this will bring to the surface the moist soil. After plowing, roll, harrow, and smooth off the surface. Mark off the rows (if the horse-hoe is to be used), twenty-one to twenty-four inches apart, and set out the plants ten inches apart in the row.

Where land is valuable, and the crop is to be hand-hoed, the rows need not be more than twelve inches apart. In fact, the better way is, to mark off the land both ways twelve inches apart, and set the plants where the lines cross. If the weather is dry, you must be very careful to press the soil firmly about the roots. Set out the plants so that the lower leaves are just above the surface. As soon as the plants get over the effects of transplanting, go through with a hoe to break the crust and kill the weeds; repeat the operation as often as necessary.

As soon as the plants are in full flower, you can begin to cut and market the crop. Where the rows are only a foot apart, the best way is to cut out every other row. Tie the sage in bunches and market it, leaving the other rows to grow larger. If the land is rich, the plants which are left will continue to grow late into the fall, and completely cover the land. After cutting out every other row, run the cultivator between the remaining rows and hoe out the weeds. Where the plants are set out in rows, twenty-one inches to two feet apart, and the land kept clean and mellow by the frequent use of the horse-hoe, the total money return is not so great as that from the double crop, but it is far less labor, and in the field-garden will be the better plan. If the sage can not be sold green in the market, tie it up into bunches and let it dry; it can then be safely shipped to any distance.

THYME.

The cultivation of Thyme is similar to that of Sage. The seeds are smaller and the plants not quite so vigorous. The soil where the seed is sown should be made even richer and finer than for Sage, and the seed must not be covered more than an eighth of an inch deep, and the bed well patted with the back of the spade. In all other respects Thyme may be treated precisely as Sage. If preferred, the seed may be sown where the plants are intended to remain. Sow in rows twenty-one inches apart, and drill in the seed as shallow as possible, dropping three or four seeds to each inch of row. It will be necessary to mix the seed with three or four times its bulk of fine dry sand, or the drill

Fig. 29.—THYME.

will sow it too thick. Cultivate and hoe, and as the plants begin to crowd, thin them out. These young plants can be drawn out by the roots, and put in bunches for home use, or for market. This thinning out can be continued at different times until the plants are left from eight to ten inches apart in the row.

In England, it is thought that thyme must be grown on the poorest of poor land, else it will lack the desired flavor. In our dry, hot climate, however, thyme will stand rich land and good cultivation. There are two kinds; one is what the European seed catalogues call "Hardy Winter," or "Evergreen." The leaves are lemon-scented, and by some it is preferred to the common, or Broad-leaved kind. Both can be grown from seed, or propagated by division of the roots, but better plants are obtained from seed. The seeds are exceedingly small, and must be sown on the best prepared and finest land. They come up slowly, and it is desirable to sow them thickly. It will do no harm if you have to thin out fifty plants to one that is ultimately left. One pound of seed to the acre will be amply sufficient.

Thyme is put up in bunches and marketed like sage, or it may be dried and shipped to any distance. Any one who has an evaporator for drying fruit, could easily devise a plan for drying bunches of sweet herbs, and make the business highly profitable.

SUMMER SAVORY.

There are two kinds of Savory; a Winter, or perennial, and the Summer, or annual sort; the latter is the best. The seed may be sown in March, in a box in the house, and the plants set out in the garden as soon as the weather will permit. This is not necessary, however, as the plants will do well if the seed is sown in any good garden soil early in the spring, or as soon as the ground and weather are warm. If it is intended to transplant the plants, sow the seed in rows, wide enough apart to admit the use of a narrow hoe, or, if the plants are to remain where the seed is sown, sow in rows fifteen inches apart, and thin out the plants enough to admit the use of a hoe. The seed should not be covered more than a quarter of an inch deep, and if the ground is moist, the shallower the better. Drop five or six seeds to the inch of row, as the thicker you sow, the easier it is to hoe between the rows of plants just before they are cracking the ground, and to keep the bed free from weeds. Four pounds of seed will be amply sufficient for an acre. If grown by the acre, I would sow in rows, from twenty-one to twenty-four inches apart, and cultivate with a horse-hoe, and thin out the plants as recommended for thyme.

Fig. 30.—SUMMER SAVORY.

SWEET MARJORAM.

The cultivation of Sweet Marjoram is precisely similar to that of Summer Savory, except, perhaps, that the plants do not bear transplantation so well, and consequently it is better to sow the seed where they are intended to remain, in rows fifteen inches apart. Sow a plenty of seed, say four or five seeds to each inch of row, and ultimately thin out the plants to ten inches apart; or, the rows may be sown twenty-one to twenty-four inches apart, and in this case, the plants may be left thicker in the row, or just wide enough apart to admit the use of a narrow hoe. If too thick, every second plant may be drawn out for early use.

7

BORAGE.

Fig. 31.—BORAGE.

Borage is not extensively grown in this country, and there is little or no demand for it in market. The seeds are large and can be sown in the open ground in rows, fifteen inches apart, dropping one to each inch of row.

Borage can be profitably grown for plowing under as a green crop. The leaves are so rich in nitrate of potash or saltpetre, that when dry they will burn like touch-paper. Borage is used only in the green state, and principally for flavoring cooling beverages, like lemonade.

ROSEMARY.

Rosemary should be sown in rows about fifteen inches apart each way. The better plan is, to drop five or six seeds in each hill, thinning out to a single plant before the plants begin to crowd each other. Cover the seed about a quarter of an inch deep.

CORIANDER.

The young tender leaves of Coriander are used in salads and for flavoring soups. The plant is easily cultivated. The seeds are round and nearly as large as a Sweet Pea. Sow in rows fifteen inches apart, dropping the seeds about an inch apart in the row, cover-

Fig. 32.—ROSEMARY.

ing half an inch deep. Light sandy soil is best for this crop; thin out the plants for use before they begin to crowd each other, ultimately leaving them seven or eight inches apart in the row. The plants soon run up to seed, and it is best to sow at intervals of three or four weeks for succession.

FENNEL.

This plant is closely related to, and can be grown as directed for Coriander.

LAVENDER.

Lavender is grown solely for its perfume. For home use, the long stems, five or six inches in length, are cut from the bushes when in flower, tied in small bunches and dried. The flowers and stems are placed in drawers, or closets among table-linen, clothing, etc. The plants are easily grown from seed, or they may be propagated by dividing the roots of old plants. It is better to grow them from seed.

Sow the seed in a box in the house about the middle of March, in rows one inch apart, dropping two or three seeds to each inch of row. If the plants begin to crowd each other before it is time to set them out in the open ground, transplant into a larger box, pricking them out to two or three inches apart each way. These strong, stocky plants, after hardening off, should be set out on loose, warm, sandy soil, in the garden, from fifteen to twenty inches apart each way. The younger and weaker plants, if the weather is warm, might be set out in a bed in the garden in rows ten inches apart and two or three inches apart in the row. In this bed they may be allowed to remain until the following spring, when they can be taken up with a good ball of earth and set out wherever there is room for them in the flower beds, or in rows two feet apart and from fifteen to twenty inches apart in the row. Lavender will in time be extensively grown in this country.

CARAWAY.

The seeds of Caraway are sometimes introduced into cheese and mixed with bread, cake, cookies, etc. The leaves, when young, are sometimes used for flavoring soups and salads. The plants are easily grown, and may be treated as recommended for Coriander.

WORMWOOD.

Wormwood is perhaps not entitled to be called a sweet herb, but it is certainly a very useful plant, and should be grown in every farmer's garden. For sprains, wormwood and vinegar is a time-honored remedy. The leaves are chopped up with Rue and Cress, and mixed with the food of young turkies. An infusion of Wormwood seeds with Chamomile flowers, is often taken as a tonic. Wormwood can be sown in a warm border early in April, in rows fifteen inches apart, and thinned to ten inches apart in the row. Next year every second plant may be dug up for transplanting, and still leave those on the original bed thick enough. If the plants are dug up with a good ball of earth their growth will not be checked.

RUE.

This very old-fashioned medicinal plant can be grown in the same way as Wormwood.

ANISE.

Anise does not transplant readily, and the seed should be sown where it is intended that the plants shall remain, in drills fifteen inches apart, dropping two seeds to each inch of row, and covering half an inch deep. The plants may be thinned out to five or six inches apart in the row.

BASIL.

Start the seeds in a box in the house, or if this is not convenient, sow in a warm border in rows twelve inches apart, dropping two or three seeds to each inch of row. The plants can be used when two or three inches high. Thin out for use until the plants are left seven or eight inches apart in the row. The leaves have a strong clove-like odor, and are used in soups and salads.

DILL.

This can be grown in the way recommended for Basil. It delights in a warm, dry, sandy soil.

CULTIVATION OF FLOWERS.

Some people think, or rather they say, that it does not pay to cultivate flowers. Whatever they may say, I do not believe that they really think so. If they do, they are certainly mistaken. It pays wonderfully well—just as it pays to be clean and neat, kind and polite. It is not necessary to argue the question. I feel sure that my young friends love flowers, and my business is to tell how to grow them with the least trouble and expense, in the greatest perfection and profusion. For my own part, I would rather see them in profusion than in perfection. I do not care how perfect they are, but I want a good many of them; this is especially true of annual flowers, or flowers grown every year from seeds. We will talk about them in alphabetical order.

ALYSSUM.

Sweet Alyssum, as it is usually called, is a very hardy plant, growing about six inches high with clusters of small white flowers, decidedly fragrant and very pretty. Sow the seeds of this plant as soon as the frost is out of the ground in the spring, in rows wide enough apart to admit the use of a hoe. Drop three or four seeds to each inch of row, and after the plants are fairly started, thin out to one or two inches apart. Keep the ground well hoed and free

Fig. 33.—SWEET ALYSSUM.

from weeds, the plant is so hardy that it is not necessary to sow the seed in the hot-bed.

AGERATUM.

This is a useful flower for bouquets, and very robust, some of the varieties growing two feet high, and producing a great abundance of white or lavender-colored flowers. Sow a few seeds in a box in the house, and set out the plants fifteen to twenty inches apart as soon as the weather will permit.

ABRONIA.

Abronia umbellata, the species most cultivated, is a Californian plant, trailing along on the ground, and somewhat resembling the Verbena. It has fragrant lilac and rose-colored flowers, which are very abundant, and continue in bloom until cut down by frost. Sow the seed in a hot-bed or in a box in the house, and set out the plants fifteen inches apart, as recommended elsewhere for Drummond's Phlox.

AGROSTEMMA.

The annual Agrostemmas are sometimes called, I do not know why, "The Rose of Heaven." The roses of earth are much more beautiful. Still the annual Agrostemma is a hardy, free blooming plant, with pretty flowers, somewhat resembling our old-fashioned pinks. Cultivation similar to Phlox.

ASPERULA.

This is a hardy annual, growing about ten inches high; a profuse bloomer, with fragrant, and pretty lavender-colored flowers, in clusters. Cultivate the same as Sweet Alyssum.

ASTERS—CHINA.

We have now China Asters as large and handsome, as double, and as perfect as the Dahlia. I know of no annual flower that has been so wonderfully improved as this, during the past twenty-five years. No garden should be without its bed of Asters. You can not have too many of them; they are in full bloom in autumn, when most other flowers have disappeared, and they continue in perfection until cut down by frost. The cultivation of Asters presents no difficulties that may not be readily overcome by the exercise of a little patience and skill. Asters can be transplanted readily, and, if convenient, can be sown in a box in the house, in rows an inch and a half or two inches apart, and two or three seeds to each inch of row; cover very lightly with fine soil, or sifted dry moss. When the plants begin to crowd, prick them out into other boxes, or into a cold frame, giving them

Fig. 34.—ASTER—PÆONY-FLOWERED.

more room. The oftener they are transplanted, and the more room you give them, the more stocky and better will be the plants. As soon as the weather becomes settled, and the soil is warm and in fine condition, set out in the bed or border, watering the plants before taking them up, until the soil is thoroughly saturated. Do not pull up the plants, but take them up with a hand-fork or trowel, and with the fingers pressing the moist earth into a ball around the roots, set them in the ground up to the lower leaves, and if the weather is dry, press the soil firmly around the roots. If the soil is moist, it must not be pressed so firmly around the roots. The proper distance apart depends on the variety; I usually plant the large

Fig. 35.—ASTER FLOWER.

kinds fifteen inches apart each way; the smaller, or dwarf varieties, should be planted in rows fifteen inches apart, and every seven and a half inches in the row. Keep the ground entirely free from weeds by the constant use of the hoe or rake. During a severe drouth, the ground may be mulched with the clippings of the lawn. Watering with a solution of superphosphate, say one tablespoonful to a gallon of water, will prove beneficial.

The varieties of Asters are numerous, and can be raised true from seed. The lamented Darwin states that he procured packets of twenty-five named varieties of common and quilled Asters, and raised one hundred and twenty-four plants, of which all except ten were true; many of the sub-varieties, however, so closely resemble each other, that it is not worth while trying to keep them distinct. Asters may be divided into three classes: the tall-growing kinds, of which Truffaut's Pæony-flowered Perfection, and New Rose, are well known, and excellent varieties. The plants of these grow about two feet in

Fig. 36.—DWARF BOUQUET ASTER.

height, and it is desirable to tie them to stakes, as they are liable to be broken during a high wind. There is a medium class, growing about fifteen inches high; one of the best of these is New Chrysanthemum-flowered Dwarf. The third class is a dwarf kind, consisting of a pyramidal mass of flowers with a few leaves at the base near the ground. Some think they are very beautiful. They range from five to ten inches in height, and go by the name of "Dwarf Bouquet Asters."

BALSAMS.

Like the Aster, the Balsam has been greatly improved. It was formerly called Lady's Slipper, from the shape of the flower; the plant was large and coarse, and had little to recommend it, except the green, healthy appearance of the foliage, and the vigor of its growth. When

Fig. 37.—BALSAMS—PLANTS AND FLOWERS.

you wish to improve a plant, or animal, native vigor, or healthy growth, is one of the essential points to start with. If you wished to whittle a doll out of a piece of pine wood, the original stick ought to be a good deal larger than the doll, so that there may be an opportunity to make it into the desired form, by cutting away the superfluous parts. So it is in improving a plant; we make it smaller and more beautiful by breeding off what we do not want, and encouraging the development and growth of those parts which we desire. The Balsam of to-day has branches and leaves so much smaller and finer than those of the old-fashioned Lady's Slipper, that our great-grandmothers would hardly recognize the plant, the flowers of which are much larger and more handsome than formerly. The Balsam still retains much of its native vigor; it is a healthy, hardy, clean-looking annual; it is transplanted easily, and is a good plant of which to sow a few seeds, [selecting, of course, the choicest varieties,] in a box in the house, and treat the plants as recommended for Asters. With Balsams, as with Asters, it is desirable to get good, stocky plants, and the oftener we transplant them when young, and the more room we give them, the more satisfaction will they give us when set out in the garden. The seed can be sown in the open ground where the plants are to remain, or it may be sown in a warm border, in rows wide enough apart to admit the use of a narrow hoe. Drop two or three seeds to each inch of row, and cover as lightly as possible, if the ground is moist. If the soil is dry, press down the soil after the seed is sown, by patting the whole surface of the bed with the back of the spade. As soon as the plants appear, hoe lightly between the rows, pulling out all the weeds, and if any of the plants are too thick in some parts of the row, transplant them, either into a new row, or to the first row when there are not enough plants. It is very desirable not to have them too thick, for, as already said, strong, stocky plants are wanted there, and you cannot have such unless they have plenty of room in which to grow. It is not necessary to plant Balsams in a bed by themselves; they look quite as well when set out separately, as when massed together. If there is any part of the flower garden where you do not know what else to set out, put in a Balsam.

The Balsam is a hardy, vigorous plant, and will do well if sown in the open ground, where it is intended to remain, but you will get much finer flowers by sowing early and transplanting frequently. Frequent transplanting checks the vigorous growth of the branches and favors the development of the flowers. The branches may be pinched off, and the plant trained to sticks, or to a trellis in any desired form, as shown in the illustrations on page 155. If planted in a bed by themselves, Balsams should be set out in rows, fifteen to eighteen inches apart, and from ten to eighteen inches apart in the row. My own plan is, to set them fifteen inches apart each way. There are many varieties of Balsams, but, except for the professional florist, the three following varieties are most likely to give general satisfaction: Camellia-flowered, in mixed colors; Rose-flowered, double, in mixed colors; Extra-double-dwarf, mixed colors.

BARTONIA.

The *Bartonia aurea,* or Golden Bartonia, is a native of California. The plant is about eighteen inches high, the numerous large and showy bright yellow flowers having a metallic lustre. The seed should be sown in the open ground, in rich soil that has been heavily manured and thoroughly prepared the autumn previous. Sow as early in the spring as the ground is in good condition, in rows fifteen inches apart, dropping a seed every two or three inches in the row. The plants are not transplanted readily, and it is best to sow where they are intended to remain. Hoe lightly and frequently, between the rows, and keep the bed entirely free from weeds. In a severe drouth, it would be well to mulch the soil, between the rows, with the clippings of the lawn.

BRACHYCOME.

The Brachycome (*B. iberidifolia*) is an Australian plant, found on the banks of Swan River, and popularly called the "Swan River Daisy." It grows about eight inches high, and produces an abundance of flowers. For the first eight years after its introduction there was no variation in the color or character of its flowers; but we have now two distinct varieties, one pure white and the other rose-colored. This is a useful edging plant to sow around the borders of a bed, leaving the plants four or five inches apart. It deserves far more attention than it has yet received.

CANDYTUFT.

Candytuft can be sown either in spring or in autumn. It is a very hardy plant, easily grown, and a general favorite. I like to see a large bed of it sown early in spring in

Fig. 38.—CANDYTUFT.

rows one foot apart, and the seeds sown quite thickly in the row—say three or four seeds to the inch. By the middle of June, the flowers will begin to show themselves, and will continue to flower for several weeks. This is a very easy and a very common method of growing Candytuft. Finer plants and larger flowers can be grown by giving the plants more room, and they will continue much longer in bloom. Candytuft can be readily transplanted, and a good plan is, to set them out in rows nine inches apart each way ; the land should be rich and kept entirely free from weeds. Candytuft is not only very pretty but it is very sweet; you cannot have too much of it in the house, and for the good of the plants you cannot cut off the flowers too frequently. If you allow it to go to seed the plant is soon exhausted, and the way to prevent this is to cut the flowers as fast as they appear.

I have heard people say that they raised flowers not for bouquets, or for use in the house, but because they wanted to see them in the garden. I have a dim recollection of making some such remark myself, when I was a boy, and did not know any better. Now, I like to see flowers in the house ; in the parlor, in the library, or on the dining-room table, anywhere and everywhere. But if one prefers to have them in the garden, if he does not care about cutting them, but would rather let them grow, there is no objection. In this case, Candytuft should be sown in succession, say as early as possible in spring, and then at intervals of two weeks, until the first of July. Again in August and September, sow a bed in a sheltered portion of the garden, where the plants can remain all the winter.

There are numerous varieties; the Pure White being the most popular. It is fragrant and a profuse bloomer. Carminia is a new variety which bids fair to be a decided acquisition. These, with the Sweet-scented Pure White, from carefully grown seed, are all that will be needed, except by the professional florist.

CALENDULA, OR POT-MARIGOLD.

The Pot-Marigolds are well-known and popular flowers. They have been greatly improved, and some of the new varieties are decidedly superior to the old kind. Cultivation similar to that of Phlox Drummondii.

COREOPSIS, OR CALLIOPSIS.

The Coreopsis is a hardy, easily grown and very showy flower. It is best to sow the seeds in a bed by themselves, in rows fifteen inches apart, and thin the plants to three or four inches apart in the rows. The flowers are on slender foot-stalks over two feet high. The soil can not be made too rich, or kept too clean, as much of the beauty of the bed will depend on having the plants strong and vigorous. A weedy, poverty-stricken bed of Coreopsis presents a sorry appearance, but if the plants are well grown the bed will be very showy and attractive.

CANNA—INDIAN SHOT.

The Cannas are now attracting much attention; being large, vigorous growing plants. Some of the varieties attain the height of five or six feet, or even more, with broad, long leaves, which look fresh and beautiful in our hot and dusty weather. A fine bed of well-grown Cannas is very pleasant to the eye, and even a single plant is very attractive.

The Canna can be grown from seed the first year, but to get fine, large plants the first season, it is necessary to sow the seed in a hot-bed or in a box in the house in March, and transplant into larger boxes, as soon as they begin to crowd; if the plants do well, they will soon need transplanting a second time, and by far the better way is, to pot them and place the pots in a hot-bed, not forgetting to plunge them well into the soil. Cannas will stand considerable heat, but ventilation and watering must not neglected.

The soil selected for Cannas in the garden should be made very fine and mellow, with a large quantity of leaf-mould, or manure, thoroughly worked into it. If the plants are doing well in the hot-bed do not be in a hurry to remove them. Set out the plants from eighteen inches to two feet apart, each way. They should have plenty of room, and the ground be kept carefully hoed and free from weeds, and it will be well to mulch the surface with litter, or the clippings of the lawn. In autumn take up the roots, and pack them away in dry sand for the winter. Set them out again in the spring and they will produce very fine plants.

CALLIRRHOË.

The cultivation of the annual Callirrhoë (*C. pedata*) is similar to that of Drummond's Phlox; it may be sown in the open ground where it is intended to remain, or the plants may be started in the house and set out fifteen inches apart. A large bed of them, if the soil is rich and the plants vigorous and healthy, is very showy. The plants commence to bloom early and continue to produce their purple flowers until cut down by frost.

CATCHFLY.

The cultivation of the Catchfly is very similar to that recommended for Candytuft. It is a hardy plant, growing about a foot high, a free bloomer; a well-grown bed of it is very attractive. The plants require rich land and clean culture.

COCKSCOMB—CELOSIA.

The Celosia, or Cockscomb, is a very interesting and attractive, though not particularly beautiful plant. The flower-stem, instead of growing erect, assumes the form of a cock's comb, and in the hands of skillful gardeners, with the aid of high manuring, this fasciated compound flower-stem attains an enormous size. One was exhibited in London eighteen inches in breadth. To attain any thing like this size, the plants should be started early and set out in the richest of soil. The plants may be grown as recommended for Asters; except that when set out in the garden, they should be allowed more room to spread themselves. If the object is to grow as large flowers as possible, the more room you give the plants the better. Ordinarily the plants may be set out from two and one half to three feet apart.

CONVOLVULUS, OR MORNING GLORY.

We have two kinds of Morning Glory; one is a climbing plant, growing with great rapidity, and throwing out a constant succession of flowers. The other is a dwarf

Fig. 39.—DWARF CONVOLVULUS, FLOWER AND PLANT.

plant. If we were speaking of beans, we should call one the pole kind, and the other the bush kind. The botanist has called one *Ipomœa purpurea*, and the other *Convolvulus tricolor*. The first named is a very rapid-growing climber, and can often be advantageously used to hide some unsightly spot or building. The trellis, poles, or strings, should be provided as soon as the plants commence to run, so that they may cling to them from the start. The soil can hardly be made too rich. If the soil is rich enough, and the surface of the land for several feet around is kept free from weeds, you may have three or four plants to each foot of trellis. During the heat of the day, the flowers are closed, but early in the morning they are out in full bloom, and are seen in all their glory.

Convolvulus tricolor, is a dwarf or bush *Convolvulus;* a bed of it, when well grown, is very showy and attractive. It is a good plan to plant the seed in hills fifteen inches apart, putting four seeds in each hill. It is generally recommended to plant them much farther apart, but I like to see the bed fully occupied.

DIANTHUS.

The genus *Dianthus* includes several of our most popular flowers, such as the Sweet William, the Carnation, the Picotee, and the common garden Pink. The kinds most easily grown from seed, and which are at the same time desirable in every garden, are the *Dianthus Chinensis*, and *Dianthus Heddewigii*, or Japanese Pinks; both can be easily grown from seed; but if not sown until May or June, in the open ground, the plants will give but few flowers the first summer. Indeed, it is better in this case not to let them flower at all, but to aim to grow strong plants for flowering the second season. They will stand the winter well, especially if protected with branches of evergreens or a light covering of horse litter.

For flowering the first summer, the plants should be grown in the hot-bed or in a box in the house. Sow the seed as recommended for Asters, and when the plants are strong and the weather warm, transplant them into a very rich, well-prepared border, from ten to fifteen inches apart. If you have dwarf varieties, they may be set seven or eight inches apart, or nearly wide enough apart to admit the use of a narrow hoe. I mention this, because it is exceedingly important to keep the soil well stirred and entirely free from weeds. The plants will flower all summer, and it is absolutely necessary to have the soil very rich, or this profuse production of flowers will weaken the young plants. If the plants do not grow vigorously, pinch off the flower-buds, and water the bed with water containing an ounce, or about a tablespoonful of superphosphate to a gallon, applying a gallon of this solution to a dozen plants. The dose may be repeated in two weeks; more than this will not be necessary, though another dose will do no harm.

DELPHINIUM, OR LARKSPUR.

The Rocket Larkspur is a well-known and popular flower, easily grown from seed. But as it is not transplanted very readily, and has to be sown in the open ground, where the plants are to remain, it does not make as large a growth as it would if it could be started in a hot-bed. Sow the seed in a well-prepared border as early in the spring as the ground can be got into good condition. Sow in rows a foot apart, and thin out the plants to four or five inches apart in the row. Keep the ground clean, and water with a little superphosphate water, as directed for the Pinks. Or what will perhaps be just as well in this case, sow from one to two ounces, or one to two tablespoonfuls, of superphosphate to each square yard of bed at the time of sowing the seed, or at any time afterwards, when there is a prospect of a good soaking rain.

The Branching Larkspur requires more room than the Rocket Larkspur, and the plants should be set from twelve to fifteen inches apart. All the Larkspurs require a deep, rich, moist soil. They do better on the north side of a slope, where they are shaded, rather than in the full blaze of our hot sun.

DIGITALIS, OR FOXGLOVE.

The Digitalis, or Foxglove, is not an annual, but is easily grown from seed, and deserves to be more generally cultivated than it now is. The plant throws up several flower-stems, two or three feet in height, each stem being covered at its upper portion with a dozen or more large, well-shaped flowers.

The seeds may be sown in a hot-bed, or in a box in the house, or in the open ground, but in the latter case no flowers will be obtained the first year, or, if the plants throw up any flower-stalks they should be cut off; the next year the plants will be strong, and produce a great profusion of flowers. In the following autumn, or spring, the roots of the plant may be divided, and in this way you will soon have all the Foxgloves you require. The plants may be set out the first year, from twelve to fifteen inches apart, but the second year they will be thick enough if they stand two to three feet apart.

DOLICHOS, OR HYACINTH-BEAN.

The cultivation of this beautiful climber is similar to that recommended for the Lima-bean. The plant grows even taller than the Scarlet Runner, but it is not so hardy; it delights in our hot sun, and should be planted in the warmest and driest soil. Like all rapid-growing plants, it requires an abundance of food, and the soil cannot be too liberally manured.

GILIA TRICOLOR AND OTHERS.

The children will all like the Gilias, if for no other reason than because they come so soon into flower. The seed may be sown in a box in the house, by the middle of March, and the plants transplanted as soon as the weather will permit; they do not bear transplanting readily, except when young. Sometimes a few of the plants will flower in the box before you are ready to set them out.

Perhaps the better way is, to sow the seeds in rings in the garden. If you take a common two-tined fork you can make a circle, in the circumference of which sow the Gilia seeds, dropping them from an inch and a half to two inches apart, in the mark made by the fork. If you use a three-tined fork you can make two rings. Sow the seed in both rings, two or three inches apart.

HELIANTHUS, OR SUNFLOWER.

My young friends must not fail to sow a few Sunflower seeds. They come up so soon, and grow so rapidly, that the plants become objects of interest from the start. Sow three or four seeds in a hill, as you would corn, say three feet apart, and thin out to two plants in a hill. Or plant a hill in any vacant spot or corner. You may plant a row along the fence, being careful, however, to leave space enough between the Sunflowers and the fence to admit of the use of the cultivator, or the hoe; thin out the plants to a foot apart. The Sunflower delights in a rich soil and an abundance of sunshine. It is a coarse plant, but is not without its attractions. The single varieties are more vigorous and, of course, produce much more seed than the double sorts. The seed is much relished by poultry. It is usually sown about the time we plant corn, but it may be put in at any time in the spring, as it is not injured by frost. See Sunflower, Double.

KAULFUSSIA.

An attractive little plant, coming very early into flower, but not lasting long. It is hardy. Sow a few circles of them, as recommended for Gilia.

LUPINES.

The Lupines are a well-known and very hardy genus of plants, belonging to the Pea family. Some of the species are grown as food for stock, and also for plowing under to enrich the land. I suppose it is called Lupine, or Wolf, because of its power to live on poor, hungry soils. Some of the Lupines are not a foot in height, while others grow on rich soil, from five to six feet high. There is a great variety of colors. The Lupine has a long tap-root, and gets its food from the sub-soil. It does not transplant easily, and should be sown where it is intended to remain. The Dwarf varieties can be sown in rings, like Gilias; the larger sorts should be sown in rows, fifteen inches to two feet apart, dropping three or four seeds in each hill, and thin out to single plants, after they are fairly established.

MALOPE.

The *Malope grandiflora* has a very large, showy flower; the plant is hardy, and vigorous, growing about three feet high. The seed may be sown in a box in the house, and the plants set out as soon as the weather is suitable, in the open ground, fifteen inches to two feet apart. The seed can be sown in the open ground, and make equally good plants, but not so early.

MIGNONETTE.

The children should get half a dozen packets of Mignonette seed with which to experiment. Let them sow a little seed when they like, where they like, and how they like. Wherever there is a little soil, two or three inches in depth, they can grow Mignonette. It will not grow in the oven or on top of the stove, because it is too hot; it will not grow in a dark cellar, because it requires light; it will not grow in the refrigerator, because it is too cold; it will not grow in the ash-pit, because it is too dry. But wherever there is a little fine, mellow soil, and it can be kept moist, in a moderately warm place, with more or less sunshine, especially more, there you can grow Mignonette. It does not matter whether the soil is in a beautiful flowerpot, or in an old tin can with a hole in the bottom. But of course while Mignonette will grow under adverse conditions, it is better to have everything connected with flowers neat and orderly; the more simple, the better. A good plan is, to fill a box, a foot wide, three inches deep, and just long enough to go upon a window-sill, fasten it with wire at the southern or eastern window, in the kitchen, or in some room where it never freezes. Fill the box with fine mould, or the finest and lightest soil you can get; water the soil with warm water, and sow the Mignonette seed, in rows two inches apart, and two or three seeds to each inch, sift on a little fine soil or pulverized moss, just sufficient to cover the seed. Nothing more will be necessary until the plants begin to grow. It will then be necessary to water the

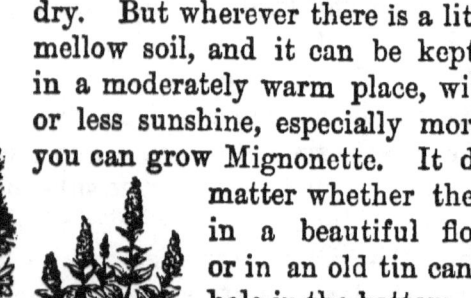

Fig. 40.—MIGNONETTE.

plants occasionally, with warm water; the hotter the room and the brighter the sun, the more rapidly the plants grow, and the oftener will they need to be watered. Before the plants begin to crowd each other, pinch a few of them off, so as to give those left room to grow.

In the open ground the bed for Mignonette should be prepared in the autumn; it should be carefully spaded, and well manured, and worked over with a hoe and rake, until it is quite fine and mellow. In the spring sow the seed on this bed, as soon as the soil is dry and the weather is warm. Unless the soil is a very light and sandy one, you must be careful not to work it when it is wet. But so soon as the soil is dry, hoe it three or four inches deep, and rake it very fine, taking off all the stones and rubbish, or dig a hole in the bed, and with a rake pull the stones and rubbish into the hole, and cover them up with fine soil. Mark the bed both ways, with a marker nine or ten inches wide, and drop three or four seeds where the lines cross each other, cover them, and if the soil is dry, pat it with the back of the spade. The seed is small, and must not be covered more than a quarter of an inch deep; if the ground is moist enough, the less covering the better. A tablespoonful of superphosphate to each square yard of bed, scattered broadcast on the surface, either before the seed is sown or afterwards, will be very beneficial.

As soon as the plants appear, hoe lightly between the rows, and all around the plants; this will leave very little weeding to be done. I recommend sowing three or four or more seeds in a hill, because the plants will come up better, and because we do not want any gaps. We do not need, however, more than one good plant in a place, and these should be far enough apart to admit the use of a hoe. If preferred, the seed can be sown in drills from eight to twelve inches apart, dropping two or three seeds to each inch of row, afterwards thinning out the plants to two or three inches apart. But the other plan will give finer plants and there is less afterwork.

Another bed should be sown a week or two later; and if the early sown bed is on warm, dry soil, facing the south, and the other bed on deep, rich soil, sloping to the north, or the north-west or north-east, you will have a longer succession of Mignonette in full flower and fragrance. The more flowers you gather, the more you will have. If you do not cut the flowers, they will go to seed and this weakens the plant; but the better way is to sow large beds at different times. Mignonette can be transplanted, but the work has to be done skillfully, and it is better to sow the seed where the plants are intended to remain. A bed of Mignonette should be sown in the autumn; this will give early flowers next spring. You can not have too many beds of Mignonette, nor can they be too large.

MIMOSA, OR SENSITIVE PLANT.

The species known as *Mimosa pudica*, or Sensitive Plant, is exceedingly interesting; it is very pretty, but its chief charm, especially to the children, lies in the fact that when you touch it, all the leaves instantly curl up, and the branch falls down.

The seed should be sown early in the spring in the hotbed or in a box in the house. When the plants begin to crowd, if the soil outside is not thoroughly warm, prick them out into a larger box, or into pots, and about the middle of June, set them out carefully in a well-prepared border. It is well to leave a few plants in four or five-inch pots. Plunge the pots in the soil so that the rims shall be even with the surface, next autumn, and before frost, remove these pots to the house. The plants will be interesting objects all winter.

MYOSOTIS, OR FORGET-ME-NOT.

The Forget-me-not requires a deep, rich, moist and mellow soil. It is best to start the plants in a hot-bed, or box in the house, though the seed may be sown in the open ground. The plants do better on a northern slope, or in a moist and somewhat shady place. The plant is perennial.

MIRABILIS, OR MARVEL OF PERU.

Make the ground very rich and mellow, sow the seeds in a row where you can hoe on each side of it, at least a foot in width. Drop a seed in each two or three inches of row, and cover by patting the soil with the back of the hoe. The plants should be thinned out to a foot apart. The plants are about two feet high, and if they have plenty of room, will throw out numerous branches. The flowers are large and fragrant, and quite showy.

THE PANSY.

The Pansy, or Heart's-ease, is not only one of the most popular, but one of the most beautiful of flowers. The improvement which has been made in the size and colors of the flowers is most marvellous. How this has been effected it is not necessary to inquire. We know this, however, that the plants, or rather the flowers, will rapidly, degenerate and decrease in size and brilliancy, when grown on poor soil, and their cultivation neglected.

If you would have the best of Pansies you must not only get seed from the best sources, but careful attention must be given to every condition of growth.

It is a very easy matter to grow really good Pansies. Pansy seed, sown last spring in a box in the house, the last of March, gave us strong plants, which, on June 25th, were flowering out of doors. Our season last year was from two to three weeks later than usual. I mention this to show that the children can, and do very readily, raise good Pansies without much weary waiting. And the beauty of it is, that these Pansies will continue to produce more and more flowers during the whole summer. The plants I speak of were transplanted two or three times, before the soil in the garden was warm enough to set them out. Early sowing, and frequent transplanting, so as to produce strong, stocky plants, is a great advantage. The Pansies are supposed to require a great deal of water. Perhaps so, perhaps not. At any rate, one of the most common mistakes, when raising

Fig. 41.—THE PANSY.

plants in the hot-bed, or in the boxes in the house, is to give them too much water. What the plants really need is, the richest of rich soils. If you want to make good coffee, you must put a good deal of coffee in the pot, and very little water. You would not get much coffee, but what you do get will be good. For my part, I would rather have half a cup of good coffee than two cups of poor. And I fancy that Pansies, to produce the largest flowers, require the richest of plant food. In other words, you must not put too much water in their coffee. The sap of the soil on which they live, should be as rich and as concentrated as you can make it. Such a soil would appear to be very moist, while in point of fact it may hold comparatively little water. It will simply hold more water during dry weather than a soil that has not been so heavily manured. The probabilities are, that this effect is produced by the formation of nitrates, by the oxidation of the nitrogenous matter in the heavily manured soil.

If this is the true explanation, what we want to produce the largest and best pansies is, first, a soil thoroughly underdrained, at least three feet deep ; secondly, a soil that is carefully spaded two feet deep and a good wheelbarrowful of manure to each square yard of ground, thoroughly worked into the soil, a foot or fifteen inches deep. Then work into the surface soil all the rich, well-rotted manure, say from an old hot-bed, you can make it hold. Few people know how much manure they can work into the soil until they set about the work in earnest. Mark you, the manure must be well incorporated with the soil with a potato hook or hoe, as you would a heap of mortar ; work it and keep working it until there is not a lump of soil, or manure left bigger than a grain of mustard seed.

On such a soil sow the seed, or set out the plants as soon as the weather is warm and settled in the spring, but it is best not to be in too great a hurry. The plants may be set out in rows nine inches apart each way. Or if preferred, plant in rows fifteen inches apart, leaving one plant every five or six inches in the row. If seed is sown in such a bed as I have described, I would sow in rows a foot apart, and drop the seeds one to two inches in the row. The drill mark should not be over half an inch deep. Cover the seed by patting the surface of the bed with the back of the spade or hoe. The varieties of Pansy are very numerous. I think my young friends will do well, at first, to sow only the choicest and best seed of mixed varieties. They may obtain plants of some of the newer varieties from the professional florists.

SWEET-PEAS.

The Sweet-pea, one of the most fragrant and beautiful of flowers, is grown precisely like other peas; it is exceedingly hardy, and grows well in a great variety of soils. To have Sweet Peas in perfection, however, three things are essential; rich land, early sowing, and the cleanest and best of culture. Perhaps it may be well to say in addition, that the plants should have plenty of room between the rows, say not less than three feet, and at the same time it is desirable to sow the peas quite thickly in the row. When thus sown, the peas come up earlier and better, and check the growth of the small weeds in the row; if you have only one row, be sure to have plenty of room on each side of the row for the use of the hoe or cultivator. I have seen Sweet-peas sown along a fence, but never knew them to do really well, because the plants were so close to the fence that they could not be hoed on both sides of the row. The peas must be provided with sticks or strings, or a trellis to cling to. I said "must be," because this is the neatest and best way, and not because the supports are absolutely necessary. In raising Sweet-peas in large quantities for seed, we do not stick them, but sow them in rows two and a half feet apart, precisely as we do common peas when growing them for market. If the ground is very rich and clean, and the soil well cultivated between the rows, you will have a finer growth and a mass of the sweetest and most beautiful flowers.

The land for Sweet-peas should be dug and heavily

manured the previous autumn, and the moment the frost is out of the ground in the spring, sow the peas, putting at least two seeds to each inch of row. An ordinary sized packet, as sent out by the seedsmen, would be about sufficient for a couple of circles some nine inches in diameter, and if this is all you intend to sow, perhaps sowing them in a circle is as good a plan as any; place a stick about three feet high, with a few branches on it, in the center of the circle for the peas to climb upon.

PETUNIA.

The Petunia has been greatly improved during the last few years, and is now one of our most popular flowers. It is easily grown, and every garden should have a large bed of it. If a few plants only are grown, to be set out singly, it is desirable to have the finest double varieties; but when massed together in a large bed, the small-flowered kinds, with more or less double ones amongst them, are exceedingly showy and pleasing. A good plan is, to prepare the bed the autumn previous, by spading and manuring; in the spring, as soon as the soil is dry and warm, hoe and rake the beds; mark off into rows a foot apart and drop four or five seeds where the lines cross. The seeds are exceedingly small, and you must be careful not to cover them too deep; if patted down with the back of

Fig. 42.—PETUNIA.

the spade, that will be sufficient covering. When the plants appear, hoe carefully between the rows and as close to the plants as you can, pulling out any weeds that may be left. As the plants grow, thin them out, and ultimately leave only one good plant in a place.

DRUMMOND'S PHLOX.

Of all annual flowers, *Phlox Drummondii* is my favorite. Although it is a native of Texas, it is admirably adapted to our climate, and every garden should have a large bed of it—the larger the better. It can be grown as easily as onions or carrots, in fact with less labor, as the plants are farther apart and nearly all the weeds can be removed with the hoe. On my farm I grow this Phlox in the field, sowing it with a garden drill, in rows twenty-one inches apart, precisely as turnips are sown. I mention this to show how easily this plant can be grown. It requires rich, clean, dry land; a sandy loam is better than either a very light sandy soil or one that approximates to a clay. For Phlox, as for many other garden crops, the true plan is to prepare the land in the autumn, making it as rich, deep, clean, and mellow as possible. The more manure you work into it, the larger and more brilliant will be the flowers, and this is especially the case if we have a dry, hot summer.

The seed should be sown as early as possible in the spring. As I said before, you ought to have a large bed of it. Single plants set out in beds with other flowers, are very pretty, but to bring out the real beauty and effectiveness of the Phlox, you should see it in large masses. If the bed has been well prepared in the autumn, as soon as it is dry and in good working condition in the spring, hoe the whole surface of the bed three or four inches deep, and work it with a potato-hook and steel rake until not a lump remains; then mark the bed into rows twelve or fifteen inches apart, and sow the seed in the rows, putting one seed to each two inches of row. This is one way; another, and I think a better plan, is, to mark the bed both ways in rows twelve or fifteen inches apart, and drop three or four seeds in each place

Fig. 43.—GROUP OF THE NEWER VARIETIES OF DRUMMOND'S PHLOX.

where the lines cross, covering not more than a quarter of an inch deep. If the soil is dry, pat it down with the back of the spade or hoe. In this case you do not need to put any soil on top of the seeds—the patting will cover them deep enough.

Only one plant is needed in a place. I recommend sowing three or four seeds, because they will come up better and quicker, and you are better able to see the plants, and hoe around them, before the weeds begin to be troublesome. Hoe frequently, and suffer not a weed to grow, and when the plants are fairly established, take out all but one in a place. Nothing more will be required, except to keep the bed entirely free from weeds.

Drummond's Phlox is so easily grown in this way that I hardly like to suggest any other method of cultivation, and before doing so, I should like to exact a promise from all my young friends, that they will sow a large bed in the way just mentioned, whether they do or do not adopt the plan I am now about to describe. The truth is, no one ever raised half enough of Drummond's Phlox, and the following plan will give you a fine lot of early plants, which you can raise to excellent purpose, while the bed grown from seed sown out of doors, will give you a glorious display of beautiful flowers, from the middle of July until cut down by frost.

This Phlox can be transplanted as easily as a cabbage, and nothing is easier than to raise a fine lot of plants in the house or hot-bed.

About the middle of March sow a box of Phlox seed in rows, one inch apart, dropping two or three seeds to each inch of row; cover the seed about a quarter of an inch deep with sifted dry moss, or less than half that depth with sifted sand, or mould. Before sowing the seed, the mould in the box should be thoroughly watered with blood-warm water. Until the plants appear, all that will be necessary to do is, to sprinkle on a little warm water to keep the surface moist; when the plants appear, especially if the room is warm, and the weather bright and sunny, they will require a little water every day. Be careful not to give too much water. Before the plants begin to crowd each other, transplant them into a larger box, or boxes, in rows two inches apart, and the plants an inch apart in the row. The soil should be thoroughly watered with warm water before setting out the plants. The box from which the plants are removed should also be saturated with warm water. Do not try to thin out the plants, but take them all up out of the box, as in this way comparatively few roots will be broken off. Of course the box from which the plants are taken can also be filled with transplanted Phlox plants.

After the plants are pricked out sift a little pulverized moss on the soil, say an eighth of an inch deep; this will check evaporation, and in a day or two the plants will be growing as vigorously as ever.

The great point after this is, to give the plants as much sunshine as possible. If kept in the shade they will be apt to grow up tall and spindling; what we want is large, stocky plants, hence they must have plenty of room. It may be necessary to transplant them once more into larger boxes, or you may remove every other row of plants, and set them out into a warm border, leaving the others to grow a little larger in the box in the house. It is necessary, in any case, to harden the plants before setting them out in the garden; this can be done by putting the boxes out of doors on a bench, on the south side of the house. At first, they should not be allowed to remain outside for more than an hour or so, during the heat of the day, gradually extending the time as the plants become stronger and more stocky.

These plants can be set out either in a large bed, in rows twelve to fifteen inches apart each way, or they may be set out singly amongst other flowers, wherever there is room for them.

The handsomest bed of Drummond's Phlox I ever saw, was on a wide outside border of a large cold grapery, sloping towards the south-west; the border had been prepared with the greatest care, and enriched for three or four feet deep with horn-piths and rich manure. From this it is evident that the Phlox, and more especially the choicest varieties, will stand high manuring; true, you can grow it on any ordinary garden soil, but it will repay all the labor bestowed in enriching and mellowing the land. The mistake most people make, is in planting too thick. On good land, twelve to fifteen inches apart each way is close enough.

The varieties are so numerous that it is hard to say which are the best. For my part, I want one pure white and one brilliant scarlet. For anything more than this I should be willing to trust to good seed of mixed varieties, from some trustworthy seed-grower.

THE POPPY.

The old-fashioned Poppy, extensively grown for the production of opium, is a hardy, vigorous-growing annual, with a white, single flower. We have, however, a number of beautiful varieties, with double flowers of all shades of color. We have also dwarf and tall varieties.

The Poppy is not transplanted readily, and it must be sown in the garden where it is intended to remain. Select the warmest and driest soil, make it fine and mellow, and sow the seed as early in the spring as the weather will permit, or about the time you plant corn.

The large Pæony-flowered Poppy has double flowers of great size and beauty. Thin out the plants to at least a foot apart. The small double Ranunculus-flowered varieties may be sown in rows about a foot apart, and thinned out to seven inches apart in the row.

If you wish to experiment in growing flowers for opium, sow in rows not less than fifteen inches apart, and thin out the plants to a sufficient distance to admit of the use of the hoe. For this purpose, the best variety is the single *Papaver somniferum*, or Opium Poppy. The time may come when the Poppy will be very extensively grown here for opium.

PORTULACA.

The Portulaca is own brother to the Purslane or "Pussley," one of the worst weeds we have on light sandy, garden soils. Both are hardy, both thrive best in sandy soils, but here the comparison ends. The Purslane is a miserable weed, the Portulaca a beautiful flower.

Fig. 44.—PORTULACA—SINGLE FLOWER.

I have heard it said that it is just as easy to raise a good thing as a bad one. Not so. The Portulaca must be cultivated with care, and the better the variety, the richer must be the soil. The double varieties of Portulaca should be sown in a box in the house about the middle of March, in rows one inch apart and two or three seeds to each inch of row. When the plants begin to crowd each other, take out every other row and set them out in another box. They are transplanted readily, and it is an easy matter to get good strong plants to set out in the garden as soon as the weather will permit.

It is of course not necessary to start the plants in the house, the seeds may be sown in the open ground. Select the warmest and lightest soil, make it as good as possible. Rake it smooth and pat it down firm with the back of the spade, then make shallow drills a foot apart and sow the seeds about an inch apart in the drill; cover not more than a quarter

Fig. 45.—PORTULACA— PLANT AND DOUBLE FLOWER.

of an inch deep. If you pat the rows with the back of the spade, this will cover the seed deep enough. If the weather is dry it will be well to water the bed occasionally until the plants are fairly started. Hoe lightly between the rows and suffer not a weed to grow. This is very important, especially when the plants are young. Thin out the plants in the row to three or four inches apart; those that are removed may be used to fill vacancies, or to make another bed.

The plants started in the house can be set out in rows a foot apart each way, and if the soil is rich enough, they will soon cover the whole bed. The great point in growing Portulaca is to get the plants fairly started; when the roots get firm hold of the soil, the hottest sun will not hurt them.

RICINUS—CASTOR-OIL BEAN.

The Ricinus, or Castor Oil-Bean, is extensively grown in some parts of this country for making castor oil. The plants grow with wonderful vigor, often attaining the height of ten feet. The leaves are large and beautiful, and the flowers of many of the varieties are brilliant and attractive. The cultivation is as simple as that of the Sun-flower or Indian Corn. Set out a plant in the centre of a bed. The Castor Oil-bean can also be used to great advantage as an ornamental screen.

SALPIGLOSSIS.

The Salpiglossis delights in a warm, sandy soil. The plants may be started in the house and set out in rows, a foot apart and five or six inches from one another in the row. The plants make a fine edging; for this purpose, make a drill around the bed nine inches from the margin, sow the seeds about an inch apart, cover lightly, hoe carefully, and thin out the plants to three or four inches apart. The dwarf variety is best for this purpose. It grows about a foot high, while the ordinary varieties are about two feet high. The flowers of both are large and showy, and are well worthy a place in every garden.

STOCKS—TEN WEEKS.

Those who have had no experience in starting flower seeds in a box in the house, would find Ten Weeks Stock a good plant to experiment with. Sow the seeds in rows an inch apart, and two or three seeds to an inch of row. Cover with a little pulverized moss, a quarter of an inch deep, or with one-eighth of an inch of sand, or mould. Give the soil in the box a thorough watering with warm water before sowing the seed; until the plants appear nothing more is required, except to sprinkle on enough water every day to keep the surface moist.

The plants of Stock can be transplanted as easily as cabbage plants, and as it is always very important to get strong, compact plants, you can not transplant them too often. As soon as the plants are an inch high, take out every other row, and prick them out into another box, and as soon as those that are left in the first box begin to crowd, if the weather is not warm enough to set them out of doors, transplant into another box in the house. If the seed is sown the middle of March, you will have strong, stocky plants, three inches high, by the middle of May. The boxes should then be placed out of doors in the sun for a few hours every day, to harden the plants.

Ten Weeks stocks are so hardy and vigorous that they will do well on any good garden soil. Set them out just as you would a cabbage plant. Put them in the ground just deep enough for the lower leaves to reach the surface of the soil. Set them a foot apart, hoe frequently, and keep the bed entirely free from weeds.

The Ten Weeks Stock delights in a moist soil and plenty of rain. But as we can not always be sure of having plenty of moisture, we should make the soil as rich as possible. This is particularly important if we expect to raise double flowers. I do not mean by this, that if we expect to grow seed that will produce double flowers, we should make the land rich. In point of fact, the seed that will produce double flowers is from plants that have been starved or dwarfed, the plants being grown with as little food and water as possible, and the seed taken from the lower half of the pod, the secondary branches of the plant only being allowed to bear seed. What I mean is, that when you have seeds grown for the special purpose of producing plants that will bear double flowers, you can not make the soil too rich for them.

SUNFLOWER—DOUBLE.

Every one knows the tall-growing, large-flowered, single Sunflower. (See page 166.) Its appearance is generally associated with unhinged gates, windows stuffed with old hats, and other marks of poverty. Nevertheless, even the common Sunflower may be so grouped as to present a striking appearance, and there is a dwarf double one that is not out of place in any garden. This has been in cultivation for many years, but no one seems to know how it originated. It has been called the "Many-flowered," the "California Double," the "Hollow Globe," and by other names. It produces small, nearly globular flowers, of a regular shape, and of a bright golden yellow color; they are without the coarseness of the single sunflower, and quite as handsome as a Dahlia. This variety is an annual.

VERBENA.

It is not at all difficult to raise good Verbena plants from seed. Sow the seeds in a box in the house, the first or second week in March. The soil can not be too rich, and it is very desirable to mix with it about one-quarter its bulk of dried and sifted moss. Before sowing the seeds, water the soil in the box with warm, or hot water, the hotter the better, provided you do not sow the seeds until two or three hours after applying the water. Sow in rows an inch apart, placing the seeds about half an inch apart on the top of moist soil, cover by scattering

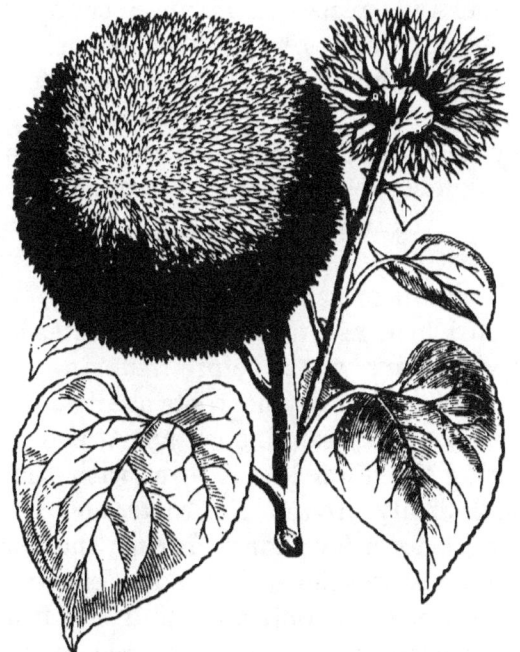

Fig. 46.—DOUBLE ANNUAL SUNFLOWER.

on dry, sifted moss, a quarter of an inch deep. Keep the box in a warm room. Very little water will be required. More plants are lost by excessive watering than from all other causes combined. As soon as the plants appear, place them in a sunny window; they grow slowly at first, and will require very little water—the warmer the room, and the brighter the sun, the more water will they need. When the plants are well out of the seed leaf, or at any rate before they begin to crowd, or to run up too tall, transplant them into a larger box, placing them at least an inch apart. The plants should not be set out in the garden until the weather is quite warm, and all danger of frost is past. If they should get too large in the boxes, it is a good plan to set them out in two-inch flower pots. Plunge the pots in a box of moist earth, or of moss, and after they have got over the check from transplanting, place them in a sunny window. Water moderately, and always with warm water, say about as warm as new milk. For a week before setting out in the open ground, the plants should be gradually hardened by placing the boxes on the south side of a building for an hour or two, during the middle of the day, and gradually extending the time until they can be left out all night with safety.

The bed for Verbenas should be a light, dry, warm soil, thoroughly enriched, and quite mellow; water the plants thoroughly with warm water before removing them from the boxes, or pots; disturb the roots as little as possible, and set them about fifteen inches apart, and just deep enough to bring the lower leaves level with the surface. Press the soil firmly around the roots, and if need be, shade the plants for a few hours during the heat of the day, until the plants recover from the effects of transplanting. Keep the bed well hoed, and free from weeds, and it will be a source of great interest and pleasure. You never know just what you will get, and it is interesting to watch the plants as they come into flower. You will be sure to have a great variety of all shades of color, and if the seeds are good, you will be certain of an ample reward for all your labor.

ZINNIA.

The Zinnia is destined to be a very popular flower. The plant is large and vigorous. The flowers are large, profuse, and brilliant. They have been wonderfully improved during the last few years, and the improvement is certain to continue year after year.

The plants can be grown in a box in the house, as they transplant with perfect safety; the oftener they are transplanted the better, as it gives us more and larger flowers in proportion to the size of the plant. Set out the plants fifteen inches to two feet apart.

If preferred, the seeds can be sown out of doors, where they are intended to remain. But a better plan is, to sow a row of them, dropping the seeds about an inch apart in the row; cover about an eighth of an inch deep, and when the plants are well out of the seed leaf, set them out in any part of the garden, where you have room for a strong, vigorous-growing plant, two feet high and two or three feet across. If the seed is good, the first flowers may not be so large or so double as those produced by the same plant later in the season.

INDEX.

Abronia	151
Ageratum	151
Agrostemma	151
Alyssum, Sweet	150
Anise	148
Asparagus	31
Asperula	151
Asters, China	152
Dwarf Bouquet	154
Chrysanthemum-flowered	154
New Rose	154
Pæony-flowered	154
Balsam	155
Bartonia	157
Basil	149
Bean, Castor-Oil	182
Bean-Hyacinth	165
Beans, Bush	36
Pole	33
Black Wax	36
Butter	36
Early Valentine	36
Golden Wax	37
Lima	33
London Horticultural	35
Speckled Cranberry	35
Scarlet Runner	36
Wax	36
White Kidney	37
Beets	37
Bassano	37–40
Dewing's Blood Turnip	40
Early Blood Turnip	38
Egyptian Blood Turnip	37
Long Smooth Red	38
Borage	146
Boxes, Window	22
Brachycome	158
Cabbages	42
Early	43
Early York	44
Flat Dutch	45
Fottler's Drumhead	44
Harris' Short-stem Drumhead	45
Henderson's Summer	44
Cabbages—Jersey Wakefield	44
Late	45
Marblehead Mammoth	45
Premium Flat Dutch	45
Savoy	47
Second Early	44
Stone-Mason	45
Winningstadt	44
Calendula	160
Calliopsis	160
Callirrhoë	161
Candytuft	158
Carminia	159
Pure White	159
Sweet-scented White	159
Canna	160
Capsicum	97
Caraway	148
Carrots	49
Early Short Horn	52
Half Long	52
Long Orange	52
White Belgian	52
Castor-Oil Bean	182
Catchfly	161
Cauliflower	47
Early Paris	48
Erfurt Earliest Dwarf	48
Lenormand	48
Walcheren	48
Celeriac	60
Celery	52
Boston Market	60
Dwarf Crimson	60
Dwarf White	60
Setting out the Plants	55
Sowing the Seed	53
Storing for Winter	58
Turnip-rooted	60
Celosia	162
China Asters	152
Cockscomb	162
Cold Frames	26
Competition in Crops	17
Convolvulus	162

INDEX.

Convolvulus, Tricolor	162	Indian Shot	166
Coreopsis	160	Insects	26
Coriander	146	Army-worm	29
Corn, Pop	64	Cabbage-worm	27
Corn Salad	65	Currant-worm	29
Corn, Sweet	61	Paris Green for	28
Crosby's Sugar	63	Potato-bug	29
Moore's Early Concord	63	Squash-bug	30
Russell's Prolific	63	Striped-bug	27
Stowell's Evergreen	63	White Hellebore for	28
Cress—Peppergrass	66	Ipomœa purpurea	162
Water	66	Japan Pink	163
Crops, Competition in	17	Kaulfussia	167
Cucumbers	69	Kohl Rabi	71
Early Frame	69	"Lady's Slipper,"	155
Green Cluster	69	Lamb's Lettuce	65
Improved Long Green	69	Larkspur	164
Russian	69	Branching	164
White Spine	69	Rocket	164
Daisy, Swan River	158	Lavender	147
Delphinium	164	Leaf Mould	22
Dianthus	163	Lettuce	72
Chinensis	163	Cos	72
Heddewigii	163	The Deacon	72
Digitalis	165	London Purple	29
Dill	149	Lupine	167
Dolichos	165	Malope	169
Drummond's Phlox	176	Mangel Wurzel	40
Egg Plant	70	Carter's Yellow Globe	41
Endive	71	Harris' Yellow Globe	41
Fennel	147	Long Red	41
Flowers, Cultivation of	150	Sutton's Yellow Globe	41
Forget-Me-Not	171	Yellow Globe	41
Foxglove	165	Manures	19
Garden, an Old and a New	8	How to Treat	11
Gardening for Boys	9	Green	12
Gardening, How to Begin	10	Marigold Pot	160
Gilia tricolor	166	Marjoram, Sweet	145
Golden Bartonia	157	Marvel of Peru	171
Green Manures	12	Melon, Musk	73
Gumbo	79	Casaba	74
Heart's-ease	171	Early Christiana	74
Helianthus	166	Green Citron	74
High Farming	15	Japanese	74
Hot-bed, to make a	25	Nutmeg	74
Hyacinth Bean	165	Melon, Water	75
Implements	21	Black Spanish	77
Acme Harrow	21	Citron	77
Gang-Plow	21	Ice Cream	77
Harrow, Acme	21	Mountain Sweet	77
Harrow, Revolving	21	Mignonette	168
Harrow, Smoothing	21	Mimosa	170
Indian Cress	78	Mirabilis	171

Morning Glory	162
Dwarf	163
Tall	162
Moss for Seeds	22
Muck, Dried	23
Mustard	77
Myosotis	171
Nasturtium	78
Okra	79
Onions	80
Early Red Globe	83
Large Red Wethersfield	83
White Globe	83
Yellow Danvers	83
Onion, Potato	88
Seed	87
Sets	86
Top	89
Tree	89
Oyster Plant	107
Pansy	171
Paris Green, To Use	28
Parsley	89
Parsnip	90
Hollow Crown	91
Long White Dutch	91
Seed	92
Peas	92
Buggy	97
Dwarf	96
Dwarf, American Wonder	96
Dwarf, Little Gem	96
Dwarf, Tom Thumb	96
Champion of England	95
Extra Early Kent	95
Kentish Invicta	95
Sweet	174
White Marrowfat	95
Pepper	97
Bell	97
Bull Nose	97
Pepper-Grass	66
Petunia	175
Phlox, Drummond's	176
Pinks, Japan	163
Poisons—London Purple	27
for Insects	27
The Care of	30
Pop Corn	64
Poppy	180
Opium	180
Pæony-flowered	180
Ranunculus-flowered	180
Potatoes	98
Beauty of Hebron	98
Early Rose	98
Early Vermont	98
Portulaca	181
Pot Marigold	160
Pumpkins	99
Connecticut Field	100
Large Cheese	100
New Jersey Sweet	100
Possum-Nose	100
Purslane	181
"Pussley,"	181
Quack-Grass, To Kill	13
Radishes—Summer	100
French Breakfast	102
Rose, Olive-shaped	102
Scarlet Turnip	102
White Turnip	102
Radishes—Winter	104
Black Spanish	105
California Mammoth White	105
Chinese Rose-colored	105
Chinese White	105
Radish Seed	102
Rhubarb	105
Cahoon's Seedling	107
Linnæus	107
Victoria	107
Ricinus	182
Rosemary	146
Rue	148
Sage	141
Salpiglossis	182
Salsify	107
Savory, Summer	144
Winter	144
Scallions	83
Sea Kale	109
Sensitive Plant	170
Soil for Seed Boxes	22
Soil, Preparation of	12
Spinach	110
Prickly-seeded	111
Round-seeded	111
Squash—Summer	112
Early Bush Crookneck	113
Early Bush Scollop	113
Squash—Winter	113
Hubbard	114
Marblehead	114
Seed	115
Starting Plants	22

INDEX.

Stocks, Ten Weeks'................183
Summer Savory............... ..144
Sunflower... 166-184
 California Double..............184
 Double........ 184
 Hollow Globe........ 184
 Many-flowered.... 184
 Single...... 166
Swan River Daisy.... 158
Sweet Alyssum.....................150
Sweet Corn........... 61
Sweet Herbs.... 141
Sweet Marjoram. 145
Sweet Peas.......... 174
Sweet Potatoes................. ... 116
 Nansemond.....................117
Ten Weeks' Stocks........... ...183
Thyme.... 143
 Broad-leaved............ 144
 Evergreen... 144
 Hardy Winter.... 144
Tomatoes............ 117
 Acme...................... 123
 General Grant.............. 123

Tomatoes, Hathaway's Excelsior..123
 Hubbard's Curled-leaf.........123
 Trophy........................123
 Raising Seed..................123
Tropæolum 78
Turnips...........................124
 Autumn............. 125-139
 Early Winter......... 126-138
 Purple Top Strap-leaf..........139
 Ruta Baga... 126
 Swedes...................... 126
 Swedes, Gathering.... 134
 Yellow Aberdeen..........126-138
Turnip-rooted Celery.............. 60
Vegetable Oyster....... 107
Verbena. 185
Watermelons........ 75
Weeds—Quack-Grass......... 13
 To Kill..... 13
White Hellebore, To Use.......... 28
Window Boxes 22
Wormwood.................... 148
Zinnia... 187

www.ingramcontent.com/pod-product-compliance
Lightning Source LLC
Chambersburg PA
CBHW020826190426
43197CB00037B/716